Behind the Songs

Graham Kendrick
with Clive Price

Augsburg Books
MINNEAPOLIS

BEHIND THE SONGS

Copyright © 2001 Graham Kendrick with Clive Price
Original edition published in English under the title BEHIND THE SONGS by Kevin Mayhew Ltd, Buxhall, England.
This edition copyright © Fortress Press 2019

All rights reserved. Except for brief quotations in critical articles or reviews, no part of this book may be reproduced in any manner without prior written permission from the publisher. Email copyright@augsburgfortress.org or write to Permissions, Fortress Press, PO Box 1209, Minneapolis, MN 55440-1209.

The publishers wish to express their gratitude to the following for permission to include copyright song texts in this publication: Kingsway's Thankyou Music, PO Box 75, Eastbourne, East Sussex, BN23 6NW, UK. Make Way Music and Ascent Music, PO Box 263, Croydon, CR9 5AP, UK. International copyright secured. All rights reserved.

All photographs are reproduced by kind permission of Make Way Music, PO Box 263, Croydon, CR9 5AP, UK. Photographs by: Walter Alexander Blisworth (p. 5), Godfrey Birtill (pp. 67, 86, 108), Hillary Brand (p. 73), Peter Honour (p. 101), Paul Bennison (pp. 114, 122), Andy Hutch (pp. 158, 184, 201, 212, 221), Howard Walker (p. 165), Harold Baruch (p. 177), Jim Loring (pp. 190, 216).

Every effort has been made to trace the owners of copyright material and we hope that no copyright has been infringed. Apology is made and pardon sought if the contrary be the case, and a correction will be made in any reprint of this book.

Cover image: Cover photo by nu1983 from iStock
Cover design: Emily Wyland

Print ISBN: 978-1-5064-5909-7

Contents

Seen on My Mantelpiece	4
Personal Tributes	6
Foreword	11
Introduction	15
Breaking of the Dawn	
The Early Singer-Songwriter Days	17
God Put a Fighter in Me	
Music from the Crucible of Experience	53
Carnival of Praise	
Taking It to the Streets	95
What Grace	
Worship for a New Millennium	159
Index of Songs	222

Seen on My Mantelpiece

Smiling shyly behind glass
    the child stands;
        fingers entwined around a small indistinct toy
            provided for distraction.
              Alongside stand older brother and sister
                  smiling down ministerially.
            Across his freckled forehead his hair lies neatly combed,
              exposing a faint frown of stifled indignation
           at being disturbed from play, scoured by a cold flannel,
            encumbered by strangely unfamiliar Sunday clothes,
              the awkward flapping at the knees,
              the large jacket's atmosphere of Sunday,
              pockets lined with fragments of sweets,
              sadly uneatable under a layer of debris
        and the worn, crumbling remnants of Sunday school drawings.
With toes curled in best sandals and
fingers disarranging with a determination of their own
all that had been arranged,
the scolding of a self-conscious mother,
the incomprehensible commands,
the manhandling into position,
the sing-song order;
    smi-all!   A click.   Smiling shyly behind glass
                                              the child stands still.

© Graham Kendrick c.1971

Personal Tributes

There are so many ways that one could make a tribute to the still ongoing work and influence of Graham Kendrick. His commitment to biblical as well as experiential inspiration could certainly be highlighted as a hallmark of his outstanding repertoire of songs. But I would like to say that this man has "raised up a highway of praise" in the nations allowing many, including myself, to journey on this route of seeing righteous praise fill the earth and heaven populated with worshippers. CHRIS BOWATER

Graham has contributed more to the church than just great songs; he's helped to teach a whole generation the glorious truths of the gospel.
STUART TOWNEND

We are so thankful that God gave us a man to work with who has demonstrated such integrity, humility, and passion for God through his lifestyle and ministry. We count it a privilege to have known Graham as a friend as well as a coworker in the ministry.
STEVE AND VELVETA THOMPSON

Even in the recording studio, Graham would continue to craft and chip away at his lyrics right up to the point of recording. LES MOIR

Personal Tributes

- The poet and hymn writer William Cowper once wrote of himself:

    "…I, who scribble rhyme
    to catch the triflers of the time,
    and tell them truths divine and clear
    which, couched in prose, they would not hear."

    It strikes me Graham's songwriting has done much the same thing for many in this generation. Every song I've ever seen of Graham's seems to be crammed full of poetic, divine, biblical truth. These songs have traveled all around the world, ushering in the revelation of God to thousands of hearts.   MATT REDMAN

- Graced and called with an outstanding gift, Graham is a master of his craft. He lives to honor Christ and serve his Church.
  DAVE BILBROUGH

- Few people get to touch a generation, fewer still touch several. Graham has made theology not just singable but memorable. Graham, we owe you a great debt. Thank you.
  WES SUTTON

- Graham has always been an experimenter with music styles and his ability to remain himself within different contexts is wonderful.
  CHRIS NORTON

- From battle cry and high praise to songs of devotion, Graham's ability to consistently resource us in worship is greatly anointed and exceptional.   TRISH MORGAN

Behind the Songs

▪ I was a 12-year-old boy when I walked into the big top at Spring Harvest for the very first time. I can still remember the feeling of electricity passing through my body as I heard this music belting out from the stage and hearing 5,000 people singing their hearts out. "Shine, Jesus, Shine" was the anthem the saints were singing, and was the moment the Church in Britain went from feeling small to thinking big. Who was this guy who spoke with such authority and churned out all these amazing anthems? I knew at that moment that this is what I wanted to do with my life and I know this book will be an ongoing inspiration for many people around the world. MARTIN SMITH

▪ I appreciate his faithfulness and integrity as a music-maker. He has impacted and will continue to impact on thousands.
SUE RINALDI

▪ Graham has been a role model for me. It has been a privilege to get to know Graham and work alongside him on so many occasions. Thanks, Graham, for being so faithful and for giving us some truly magnificent songs.
NOEL RICHARDS

▪ I believe Graham Kendrick will be recorded in heaven's history books as one who faithfully served his generation to stimulate global praise.
GERRIT GUSTAFSON

Personal Tributes

Father of the modern worship scene, Graham is a pioneer and a master craftsman anointed to restore to God's house heartfelt worship in truth and in Spirit.
RICHARD LEWIS

Graham's contribution to worship worldwide has not only been through songs but his constant willingness to encourage others.
ANDY PIERCY

Graham has been an inspiration through his passionate dedication to the Lord Jesus, and care toward those of us following in the ministry.
DAVID LYLE MORRIS

Graham's passion for the Kingdom of God, not just in word but in action, is a real inspiration to me.
BRYN HAWORTH

I look up to Graham not just as a writer of great quality, but as a spiritual elder. I remember the words he's prayed over me years later, and like his songs, they come back with power, love, and sound judgment!
IAN WHITE

Foreword

Moving to Baltimore after three years in Chicago was not an easy thing to do. The 1,200-mile relocation was one thing, but changing allegiance from one American football team to another was a different matter entirely!

However, the timing was good, for the Baltimore Ravens managed swiftly to find themselves in the Super Bowl, which is the FA Cup Final of the USA. Unfortunately, the Super Bowl coincided with a trip I had to make to Britain to preach at Ichthus Christian Fellowship. The match was due to be played during the night following this speaking engagement, and immediately prior to taking the plane back to the USA.

Unbeknown to my wife Ruth and I, Graham went searching for a suitable hotel that had a Sky Sports TV Channel, and was near the airport. He succeeded in his search, and subsequently booked a room for us where we could watch the Super Bowl. He and Jill paid the bill—and Baltimore won!

A simple gesture, but one that speaks much of Graham. After 30 years, I guess that I know him very well, and knowing Graham has been one of the single greatest privileges of my time in Christian ministry.

Many say that it's never easy to know the real person when you see them leading worship, or performing from the platform. Yet it is possible to know Graham from a distance, and the best way to do it is through his songs. For the way that Graham writes his material is to put on paper some of those lessons that God is teaching him in his life. He does it with a simple humility, and yet a profound sense of meaning surrounds the words that flow from his pen. Here in this book lies the chance of getting to know the real Graham Kendrick.

From the early years of beginning to write performance songs, to the beginnings of the worship material that were to help revolutionize our vocabulary of worship in the UK, the beginnings are well charted in this volume.

From all the time that we spent on the road together, for the many curries, the conversation, and the innumerable people we met and saw God work in their lives, those years will always have a very special place in my memory. For they were not only life-changing for some of those we met, but the time spent with Graham effectively changed my life, too. From him I learned what it meant to begin to accept myself, to forgive others for the more unfortunate chapters in my own life, and to love God in a way that I had not before understood. It's strange to confess that one owes such a debt of gratitude to another individual. But it would be less than real not to admit that being with Graham through those years was an experience that I would never have wished to miss.

Foreword

It's my hope and prayer that as you read the song lyrics, and learn of the background from which they emerged, God will touch your own life with a sense of his magnificence, glory, and desire to touch and minister to you as well.

For these were the early years when God was doing his formative work in Graham's life, laying the foundations for the ministry that would follow, teaching lessons with which it is easy for us all to identify. No one can walk another person's pathway, but all of us can learn a little of the Divine purpose by the way that God moves in the life of an individual. Telling the story through song lyrics is an unusual and very effective way of communicating—and it's the gift that God has placed in Graham's heart and life.

So welcome to a journey, and may it prove to be a great blessing to you as well. He may never pay for you to watch the Super Bowl, but in his words and music Graham has provided a legacy for the British church. Read and enjoy these wonderful lyrics and learn something of the man behind the songs.

Clive Calver
Baltimore

Introduction

Graham Kendrick's songwriting has been part of the soundtrack for much of my Christian life. Whatever I was going through, his compositions were usually somewhere in the background—comforting me, challenging me, reminding me to keep the main thing, the main thing.

I first came across his music as a teenager while living in the northwest of England. My classmates were into Pink Floyd and Deep Purple. I was into Paul Simon and Ralph McTell! A friend at church said I ought to listen to this Christian singer called Graham Kendrick. It fit the bill exactly: contemporary folk-rock with a sharp lyrical edge and honest, human poetry. "The Executioner" was a favorite, with its depth and drama.

There was a gig at Liverpool University where Graham played "Make It Soon," his song about the Second Coming. It had a deep impact on me, and on a few of my friends. We were on the leadership team of a big youth group at the time, and felt convicted about our corporate spiritual state. So we went forward for prayer. It was a powerful moment.

I remember one early Greenbelt. They called it a mudbath. The whole place got rained out. The main stage was abandoned. All the bands and artists had to set up their gear in a marquee. My friends and I managed to squeeze in near the front. Graham was on the bill that night. I remember him singing his "signature tune" "How Much Do You Think You Are Worth?" It was a great atmosphere.

Years later, I was leading worship at a church on the south coast of England.

Of course, Graham appeared again—we used several of his worship songs each week in the congregation. When I joined one of the early March for Jesus events in London, once again we were singing his material as we prayed at key "power bases."

When I finally met him at a March for Jesus celebration in Hyde Park, I plucked up the courage to tell him how much his music had meant to me. Instantly Graham changed from the confident international worship leader to a shy, sheepish bloke who didn't know how to respond to a compliment. That's what so many of us like about him.

This personal collection of songs and memories is not just Graham's story. For everyone who's laughed, cried, and stood in awe at what God has done across the Church over the past 30 years, it's your story and it's my story.

God bless you, Graham. It's been a privilege working with you on this family album.

Clive Price

May 2001

Clive Price is a freelance journalist working with a number of Christian organizations and periodicals in Britain and the USA.

He is editor of Worship Together *magazine, UK correspondent for* Charisma *magazine, author of* Glorious Awakenings *(SPCK/Triangle), and coauthor of the award-winning* Miracle Children *(Hodder & Stoughton).*

Married with three children, Clive lives in West Sussex, England.

Breaking of the Dawn
The Early Singer-Songwriter Days

Behind the Songs

Breaking of the Dawn

Long as I Live

Long as I live
    I'm going to make my heart your home
  and I will be a temple for my sweet Lord.
      Long as I've got music
    and heart and hands to raise,
      long as this old earth will hold me down.
    Don't talk to me of dying,
    I know of no such thing,
        just talk to me of Jesus,
           he's forever everything.

Graham Kendrick
© Copyright Control

Behind the Songs

After church on a Sunday night, there would often be a crowd at our house singing around the piano. My father in particular enjoyed music and had taught himself to play the piano and accordion, so he would lead the songs and choruses. When you're a kid you just listen and take it in, then after a while you experiment with harmonies and so on.

My older brother and sister began to have piano lessons. And in typical sibling rivalry fashion, I didn't want to be left out as number three in the family. So I insisted on having lessons myself. I had an ear for music and was able to learn the little exercises from the teacher—but I wasn't making the connection with the funny dots on the page. Because I was very shy and didn't want to admit that I didn't really understand what the music was about, I just played what I'd learned by ear and pretended to follow the score. The eventual result was that the teacher gave me up in complete frustration!

I guess the whole experience prejudiced me against music theory. I almost became allergic to sheet music. Years later in my teens, I yearned to play some of the music I was hearing on the radio. So I got hold of a guitar that my dad had in a closet somewhere.

I was determined not to use a book or have lessons. I would just try and teach myself. Eventually I did discover that chord charts could be quite helpful, but it set me off on the "play it by ear" method in a determined kind of way. For that reason music, in my imagination, had nothing to do with notes and staffs. I can still remember riding my bicycle on my paper route on the streets of Putney and thinking of tunes in my head. But I'd see them in colors rather than notes. It was like every pitch had a color, and I would desperately try and remember the melody in my head for when I got home.

That era was particularly interesting for the Church. It was the '60s, and youth culture suddenly burst onto the scene. But the Church as a whole was not responding to it. There were some folks who were beginning to say, "We have to relate to the youth in a way that they understand." So they put on special events—including at coffee houses. The idea was to take over a building, turn it into a low-lit, relaxed venue with seats around tables, book a band, and enlist the help of an evangelist who had some skill in communicating to young people.

Along with my brother and sister and some friends, I aspired to having a band that would operate in that situation. We couldn't just do cover versions of what was in the charts at the time, because we had a message to share. The obvious answer was to write our own material. So that's what I began doing. Almost immediately it became a passion of mine to write. I discovered I could do it, to some degree. My mother tells me it was around that time I announced that I wanted to be a professional songwriter.

It was the days of Radio Luxembourg and pirate stations like Radio Caroline. I tuned in to their programs while hidden under my sheets at night. It wasn't that the music was banned from our home. But I should have been getting some sleep to be ready for school the next day. I was listening to the Beatles, Simon and Garfunkel, the Hollies, the Searchers, Pink Floyd, Rolling Stones—anything really that was in the charts. My older brother used to buy records, which meant I got to listen to them for free.

> **Then along came these hairy hippie types... doing dance and drama. It was quite controversial. And I was one of them!**

Every Sunday I would be in church singing the traditional hymns and then listening to The Beatles when we got home—which is why when people ask me who my inspirations are, I typically say, "The Beatles and the Baptist Hymn Book." Undoubtedly my early songs were to some extent derivative of what was on the charts at the time.

Until then, evangelism tended to follow the Billy Graham—type model. Then along came these hairy hippie types playing rock music on electric guitars and doing dance and drama. It was quite controversial. And I was one of them! The whole thing was very new. It was a new generation. It was the rock "n" roll generation. This hadn't happened before. So it was a self-help kind of situation. Everyone was learning completely from scratch.

My lack of training in songwriting and blatant ignorance of compositional theory became an asset! This was the era of Lennon and McCartney. And it was almost a badge of '60s authenticity to not read music, because the only people who read music were seen as old-fashioned. The reality was that there were people working behind the scenes of the pop industry like

George Martin who knew a lot about music. But the image was, "We're just ordinary guys making up songs because that's what we like to do."

In 1969 I went to college and took an interest in contemporary folk music. I was listening to people like Simon and Garfunkel, Al Stewart, Cat Stevens, Gordon Giltrap, and John Martyn. That music was enjoying popularity, and because it had a lot of lyrical content, I was drawn to it. The folk boom saw me swapping my electric guitar for an acoustic one, and I began to write songs within that genre.

"Long as I Live" was possibly my first worship song. When the moment was right, I used to sing it in concerts. I'd link it in with the Edwin Hawkins Singers' "Oh Happy Day," which had been in the charts. So everybody knew it and enjoyed singing it. The George Harrison influence can be seen in the line, "I will be a temple for my sweet Lord." It became a simple sing-along thing. Interestingly, I used the phrase "heart and hands to raise," which hints at the physical liberation of the early days of the renewal movement!

I came from a background of very formalized religion, perhaps rather lacking in demonstrative worship. But along came these charismatics saying, "If you're going to give your whole self to God, that includes your body and if you look at the Bible, hands are raised and people kneel and people bow and people even dance." So one of the simplest expressions would be people raising hands in a gesture of openness to God. The song reflected something of that feeling.

Behind the Songs

How Much Do You Think You Are Worth?

Is a rich man worth more than a poor man?
A stranger worth less than a friend?
    Is a baby worth more than an old man?
    Your beginning worth more than your end?

    Is a president worth more than his assassin?
        Does your value decrease with your crime?
            Like when Christ took the place of Barabbas,
                would you say he was wasting his time?

        Well, how much do you think you are worth, boy?
        Will anyone stand up and say?
        Would you say that a man is worth nothing
until someone is willing to pay?

I suppose that you think you matter,
    well, how much do you matter to whom?
        It's much easier at night when with friends and bright lights
            than much later alone in your room.

        Do you think they'll miss one in a billion
        when you finish this old human race?
           Does it really make much of a difference
                when your friends have forgotten your face?

Breaking of the Dawn

If you heard that your life had been valued,
that a price had been paid on the nail,
   would you ask what was traded,
      how much and who paid it,
     who was he and what was his name?

          If you heard that his name was called Jesus
       would you say that the price was too dear?
    Held to the cross not by nails but by love,
  it was you broke his heart, not the spear!

Would you say you are worth what it cost him?
   You say "no," but the price stays the same.
     If it don't make you cry, laugh it off, pass him by,
       but just remember the day when you throw it away
         that he paid what he thought you were worth.

         How much do you think he is worth, boy?
         Will anyone stand up and say?
        Tell me, what are you willing to give him
        in return for the price that he paid?

Graham Kendrick
Copyright © 1974 Kingsway's Thankyou Music

Behind the Songs

My first major break was singing at the back of a tour bus in between concerts. I was playing guitar in a backing band on a tour organized by Musical Gospel Outreach. During those long journeys I'd get out my guitar and sing one or two songs I'd written. One of the organizers took note of my material.

An American band pulled out of one of the dates at Westminster Central Hall, leaving a gap in the program. They decided to let me do a 15-minute set, which was fortunate because I only had enough songs to fill that amount of time! It must have been a success, because they booked me as a main artist on the next tour. That gave me an immediate platform for my singer-songwriter material.

MGO were developing connections in America, where a revival was under way in the hippie culture. Thousands of young people were becoming Christians, and many of them were musicians. Then they started making albums and some found their way across the Atlantic—Love Song was one of the best known of those bands—followed later by the artists themselves. A healthy interaction was happening. So MGO arranged for me to visit the States early in 1973. It was a very low-key, *ad hoc* kind of tour.

It was terrific experience. And it was interesting to experience the revival. I went to a big circus tent in Costa Mesa, California, which later became Calvary Chapel. It was one of the key centers for the so-called "Jesus People." I went to hear one or two bands.

Hundreds of people would flock to these concerts, and I was amazed to see people just streaming to the front when they made a simple "altar call." I had come straight from England where it was so hard to get any response at all to the Gospel, and you had to be very clever and subtle in the way that you put it across. I just couldn't work out this phenomenon.

I went to see a baptism in the sea, which was one of the stereotypical scenes of the Jesus Movement days. I'd seen pictures of these mass baptisms off the California coast and found myself attending one. So far as my music was concerned, I think the Americans were totally baffled by it! It was just too subtle, too obtuse. I had a great time and met some great people, but it was obvious that the chemistry wasn't there for my material.

The revival fervor of the Jesus Movement drifted over to the UK, and I suppose in some ways we cultivated a British version of that phenomenon. People were becoming Christians at outreach events—perhaps not in their thousands as in California—but certainly in their hundreds. A new generation was emerging. Our American cousins had proved to us that you could be a Christian and have long hair and wear strange clothes. That brought a measure of freedom and inspiration, though I didn't adopt the whole package. I never had a caftan.

> **That brought a measure of freedom and inspiration, though I didn't adopt the whole package. I never had a caftan.**

It was an interesting time for us all. Some major events were drawing Christians together from across the UK. The Festival for Jesus in London attracted tens of thousands of people.

We were still in the era of big demonstrations like the anti-Vietnam protests, but to draw Christians together on a similar scale was quite new for the churches. And Christian versions of the secular rock festivals were springing up.

Among the visitors from the States was Arthur Blessitt—a long-haired hippie evangelist who carried a full-size cross with him wherever he went. Former teenybopper heartthrob Pat Boone brought the American musical *Come Together*, and it turned out to be a powerful influence on British churches. Despite the sugary ballads, it's safe to say that it literally changed the way we worshipped and brought Christians together from across the old denominational divides. It was a time when a lot seemed to be happening around the place—lots of tours and albums—and people doing new things.

I toured in my own right and recorded a few solo albums. I was at a creative peak when *Paid on the Nail* came around, and one of the tracks—"How Much Do You Think You Are Worth?"—became my signature tune for some time.

I was inspired by an illustration that Clive Calver used in his talks those days. He would describe an incident when his wife Ruth lost her wedding ring. Of course it was a major trauma until the ring was found. Clive would explain that a wedding ring might not be worth a fortune. But to the person who'd lost it—for whom it represented a romance and marriage—the ring was worth far more than its market value.

I developed that theme in a series of questions: "Is a rich man worth more than a poor man and a stranger worth less than a friend?" I wrote the song while sitting on the edge of the bed in the spare room at the Calvers' house in the West Midlands.

"How Much Do You Think You Are Worth?" soon became one of those defining moments that you build up to in a concert. I still use it today, especially when I play concerts in prisons. It has a particularly poignant quality in those situations.

Behind the Songs

Kingdom Come

I was begging in a doorway
my begging bowl in hand
    when someone said, "That joker's head
    is heavy and bowed down.
        The court has sat in anger,
        the rabble rallied round,
            the thorny-crowned King-carpenter
            was hounded out of town."

I don't believe in bayonets,
I don't believe in war,
but men shall not be free
until the Devil rides no more.
    Understand he fights for you
    and understand it well,
    hanging high his battle cry,
    will break the gates of hell.

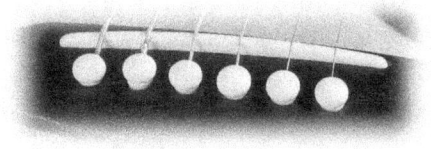

        Well, he must have been a dreamer
        with his talk of kingdom come,
    I see no bright battalions
    come flashing in the sun.
      The ridges hold no heroes
      to descend and circle round,
this lonely hill must surely be
the strangest battleground.

Breaking of the Dawn

But on his face amazing grace
is written deep in blood.
Amazing price of sacrifice
is stained upon the wood.
Can't you see he dies for you?
You see it, oh, so well,
hanging high, his battle cry
will break the gates of hell.

Well, a warring world was weary,
their begging bowls held high,
when from east to west the lightning blessed
believers in the sky.
The whole world stopped to listen
and everyone knelt down,
the King they called the carpenter,
has landed, he's come down.

And on his face amazing grace
is written deep in blood.
Amazing price of sacrifice
is stained upon the wood.
Now you know he died for you,
you know it much too well,
hanging high, his battle cry
broke the gates of hell.

Graham Kendrick
Copyright © 1973 Kingsway's Thankyou Music

I was somewhat shocked when Billy Graham got up to speak. He kicked off by quoting from a song I had just sung! The occasion was Spree 73 and the composition was "Kingdom Come," from the *Bright Side Up* album. Short for Spiritual Re-emphasis, Spree was a large-scale youth event at Earl's Court. It was the biggest venue I'd ever played.

Billy quoted the lines from the chorus—"and on his face amazing grace was written deep in blood, amazing price of sacrifice is stained upon the wood… you know he died for you, you know it much too well, hanging high, his battle cry, broke the gates of hell."

One of his staff members must have taken notes while I was singing. Sometimes these guys specifically ask the organizers what is going to happen before they go on so that they can relate back to it. Maybe he was given the song lyrics in advance. However he did it, I was absolutely thrilled that Billy Graham should quote me! It was a great endorsement for a 22-year-old starting out.

There were many thousands of young people there. It's a very optimistic time when you are in your early 20s, with a great sense of life being before you. But there was definitely a lot happening, certainly for the people of my age at the time. There was a sense of excitement and of the generation doing it their way. Musical Gospel Outreach was bringing in people like Larry Norman from the States and booking pretty significant venues such as the Albert Hall.

I was absolutely thrilled that Billy Graham should quote me! It was a great endorsement for a 22-year-old starting out.

I wrote "Kingdom Come" by imagining myself stepping into the shoes of a bystander at the time of Jesus. In this case it was a beggar, watching Jesus and trying to work out who he was and what was going on, and sifting through the differing opinions.

Although I didn't contrive it in this way, the storytelling approach turned out to be a good device for getting people to think about who Jesus was—which is obviously one of the major things you want people to grapple with when you are presenting those kinds of concerts.

I used to "top and tail" it with an acoustic guitar instrumental of "Onward Christian Soldiers" that used a lot of harmonics and so on. It added an interesting dynamic to the piece. It was one of those little attention-grabbing performance things that works well in a program, and it became something of a trademark, along with the use of percussive effects on the body of the guitar.

It also brought the idea of battle into the storytelling, seeing the crucifixion as a struggle with evil, and "Onward Christian Soldiers" has resonances with that. None of it was particularly contrived—it was just the way these things happen when you are writing a song and you suddenly find you are playing a bit of "Onward Christian Soldiers." So that was a standard for many years in my concert set.

Breaking of the Dawn

Behind the Songs

Sweet Fire

Hushed the room and silent
    when her knock came on the door,
        "Mary, you've been dreaming," I said,
            "visions come to weeping eyes
                like trouble to the poor.
                      Don't go chasing dreams among the dead."
Hushed the room and silent
    as she stood beside the door,
        "Mary, roll your tears away," I said,
            "I don't believe your story
                but I must believe your eyes.
                      Let's go chasing dreams among the dead."
So the morning found me running
    as the sun just touched the sky,
        breathless as the night was rolled away.
            I stumbled through my hopes and fears
                and found that you were gone,
                      risen like the sun to bring the day.
Lately I've been pretty near
    to heaven in his eyes.
        Lately I'm amazed that it's all true.
            I'd lost myself in sorrow
                and I couldn't find the door,
                      now I find I've lost myself in you.

Breaking of the Dawn

Suddenly I'm burning
    with a sweet and strange desire.
        Jesus, I've been dying far too long;
            my body has been waiting
                for the water and the fire,
                    home is where you are,
                        where I belong.
And now the Great Pretender
    must continue to pretend
        that he didn't fall like lightning from the sky.
            For love has found a highway
                and life has lost an end,
                    Nazareth's lost a carpenter
                        but the world has found a friend.

We weren't doing very well. The sound was pretty flat and we weren't getting much response from the audience. It was back in the pre-college coffee house days, and I was playing guitar in the band with my brother Pete and sister Gillian, our rhythm guitarist Richard, singer Margaret, and drummer Martin.

We were on the same bill as a group from a black Pentecostal church. As if rubbing salt in our wounds, one of the members of this other band spoke to us afterward and told us that we needed the Holy Spirit! We didn't take too kindly to that. The message came across with a kind of "something's wrong with you guys, there's something missing" air. And when you're an insecure young man you're very sensitive about that sort of thing. However, despite all the discomfort and difficulty of the situation, something hit home.

When I eventually went to teacher training college, I became increasingly aware that the faith I practiced didn't have quite the same zap as the Christianity I saw recorded in the New Testament. I left a particularly flat Christian Union meeting thinking, "Is this real—or are we all pretending?" I walked into the late night air, burdened by serious doubts and wondering if we were all just fooling ourselves. I prayed a simple prayer to the effect of, "God, if it is real, then show me something more than this. I want something more than this." I also remember attending a meeting at Kensington Temple and responding to an invitation for prayer to be filled with the Holy Spirit. I went home totally unmoved by the experience, yet still resolute in my search.

I began to meet a few people who claimed to have had an experience of the Holy Spirit. It seemed to be a major thing in their lives and they were absolutely full of it. So that aroused my curiosity and spiritual hunger. I asked one of them, "Where did this happen to you and how did it happen?" He'd been associated with a little church that was meeting in a home—a sort of very early house church where they believed in these kinds of things. They'd prayed for him and this amazing experience had happened. So I decided to go along and check it out.

During the summer holidays I found out the address. I knocked on this door in southwest London. There weren't many people there. We just sat round in someone's living room. One of the things I remember was this woman who had a beautiful voice. She sang extemporary in what the New Testament calls "unknown tongues." It was the most beautiful sound I'd ever heard. It was like hearing an angel sing. There was prayer and some worship, and then afterward one or two of them spoke to me, wanting to know who I was and why I was there. I received more prayer and—guess what? Nothing happened!

I returned home, wondering if God really wasn't that interested in Graham Kendrick's epic spiritual quest. However, I would still be a good boy and brush my teeth before I went to bed. So there I was in the bathroom when suddenly this strange thing started to happen to me. It felt like I was filling up from the inside, and a big smile appeared on my face! I knelt down by the bathtub as I began to overflow with a previously unknown experience of joy and the presence of God.

It had a massive impact on my life. The biggest effect was that it introduced me to worship in the Spirit—not that I hadn't been helped by the Spirit before in my worship. But now something tangible was happening inside me. It wasn't just me making up my mind to sing a hymn—it was the Spirit inside, urging me and overflowing with something that I knew didn't come from me. It launched me into a whole process of learning to worship.

These days, physical expression of worship such as raising hands is unremarkable, but at that time it was regarded as extreme—even cultic. For someone as shy and introverted as me, it was radical and potentially embarrassing. Believe me!

I spent a lot of time just shut away in my own room praying, kneeling, standing, or raising my hands—learning to worship with my whole being. You name it, I did it! I was getting free of all the inhibitions. I tend to trace much of my worship songwriting back to that time. If you're going to lead people in worship, or write worship songs, you have to be a worshipper. You can't take people where you've never been yourself.

My brave new world was reflected in "Sweet Fire," which appeared on my first album, *Footsteps on the Sea*. This story song used to be a standard part of my repertoire in the early '70s. It's the account of when Mary had been to the empty tomb, met Jesus, and returned to tell the disciples that he'd risen from the dead. The drama unfolds through the eyes of one of the disciples who runs to the tomb, so it's got to be either Peter or John. But it's more than just a story. There's some broader comment and poetry that takes it beyond just a historical account.

> "What does this all mean?..."
> At least I felt I'd stopped pretending.
> I had an experience of God that was real.

One of the verses relates back to my personal encounter with the Holy Spirit: "Suddenly I'm burning with a sweet and strange desire. Jesus, I've been dying far too long; my body has been waiting for the water and the fire, home is where you are, where I belong." They were echoes of what had been happening in my own life.

There was more lyrical depth, too. These were the days of "concept albums"; long-playing records tucked inside huge gatefold sleeves that had all the words printed on them. People loved to unravel the poetry that was inherent in some of the songs of that time. And I was writing into that whole culture. "Sweet Fire" finished with, "And now the Great Pretender must continue to pretend that he didn't fall like lightning from the sky. For love has found a highway and life has lost an end, Nazareth's lost a carpenter but the world has found a friend."

I would look out at the faces in the crowd and everyone would be taking it in and trying to work out the meaning: "What does this all mean? Who's the Great Pretender?" At least I felt I'd stopped pretending. I had an experience of God that was real.

Behind the Songs

The Executioner

I am a soldier for the Emperor,
    I am a fighter by my trade,
I've seen cruel men and heroes die.
    I've seen courage face the blade,
I've seen traitors mourn the men
    that they betrayed.
    I am a soldier for the Emperor,
believer in the wisdom of the sword,
    but the tools I use to kill
are now a scaffold and a hill,
    the rebel and the murderer's reward.

So let the women bear the standard
    and the soldier bear the child,
let the eagle carry peace upon her wings.
    Let the heroes laugh like children
    with the warriors great and wild
    now that crosses are made for kings.

    I am a soldier for the Emperor
and scars remain my only souvenirs,
    but a deeper scar than these
disturbs my night, disturbs my ease,
    when this King with sorrow
in my dream appears.

Breaking of the Dawn

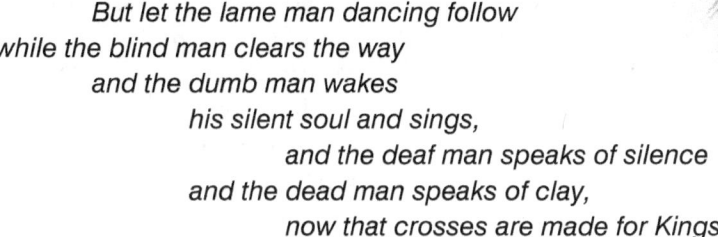

In the darkness I remain the executioner
      and I'm sure as we are standing on this hill
there's something going on up here
      that I don't understand
and I wonder if I ever really will.

      But let the lame man dancing follow
    while the blind man clears the way
     and the dumb man wakes
        his silent soul and sings,
          and the deaf man speaks of silence
      and the dead man speaks of clay,
         now that crosses are made for Kings.

      So I think I'll take my old affairs
        and bury everything,
     and I think I'll change my Emperor
        for a King.

Graham Kendrick
© Copyright Control

I can remember making a very conscious decision at about 17 that I would attempt in all my songs to avoid any kind of jargon or Christian clichés. The first result of that was the realization how little I actually understood when I tried to unpack the jargon! I also found it was quite hard to put the Christian faith in a song that didn't use clichés. So a number of songs ended up with apparently very little about the Christian faith at all!

But I also began to write songs that told a story—which is always a great way to engage people's attention. I would take biblical characters and situations and try to dramatize them in a song. That kind of material provided much of my early repertoire in the intimate atmosphere of a folk club or small concert hall. It was the age of the lone singer-songwriter who, with guitar in hand, would bare his soul before a listening audience.

One of those songs was "The Executioner," which was based on the centurion who oversaw the crucifixion and who ended up saying, "Surely this was the Son of God." The piece explains how the experience turned his world upside down. It's a very dramatic song, and was a popular favorite from the *Footsteps on the Sea* album. That was a landmark recording for me, being my first solo effort. It was an exciting time. I was only about 21 at the time and I'd been getting to know a guitarist named Gordon Giltrap who was on the folk club circuit.

Gordon used to live in the same area as the college I attended, so I used to visit his home occasionally. It was watching him perform that introduced me to open tunings on the guitar—which formed a musical basis for a lot of my songs at the time. He was quite interested in the Christian faith and agreed to play on my album. These days you'd call it "unplugged," because it was just two acoustic guitar players—myself and Gordon—and a string bass player named Chris Lawrence.

It was quite daunting going to this big London studio. We basically recorded it like a "live" concert, the only audience being the people in the control room. I think it was a very tiny budget, we were allowed only two days—and you can tell so from the album. There was no going back to re-sing something out of tune!

We basically recorded it like a "live" concert…we were allowed only two days—and you can tell so from the album. There was no going back to re-sing something out of tune!

Behind the Songs

Peter at the Breaking of the Bread

Well, I was standing in the shadows
    at the breaking of the bread,
    as he touched the cup in silence
    at the bowing of his head,
    and Judas stole out silently
    as hushed the prayers were said.
    I knew this was Jesus
    at the breaking of the bread.

    Well, I was standing in the shadows
        of the cool Gethsemane,
        trying hard to disbelieve
        What my weary eyes could clearly see.
        The lights, the cries, the flash of steel,
        in the shadow of an outstretched tree.
        I knew this was Jesus
        but this I could not foresee.

        I was standing in the shadows
            as the prisoner was led,
            trying not to tremble
            at the turning of his head,
            trying not to notice
            at the breaking of his heart.
            I knew this was Jesus
            and soon he will be dead.

Breaking of the Dawn

I was standing in the shadows
    at the throwing of the dice,
    wishing I was twenty thousand men,
    man, I would take that soldier's life.
    But Jesus looked down quietly,
    forgiveness in his eyes.
    I knew this was Jesus,
    such love comes as a surprise.

        Well, I was standing in the shadows,
            man, I wished I'd not been born,
            rubbing shoulders with the soldier boys
            who laughed and mocked to scorn my Lord.
            I could hardly recognize his face,
            his body was so torn,
            I knew this was Jesus
            and soon he will be dead.

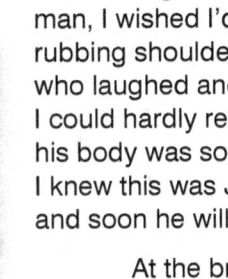

                At the breaking of the dawn
                    I stood and watched the place
                    where they laid his body down,
                    but on the stone bed, where they laid him dead,
                    no body could be found.
                    Then a man in white, a dazzling sight
                    with a voice of triumph said:
                    'He is alive! He is alive!
                    He is alive! He is alive!'

Graham Kendrick
Copyright © 1976 Kingsway's Thankyou Music

Behind the Songs

Bright Side Up—album number two—marked a move away from the purely "unplugged" sound toward a more commercial pop style. There's clearly a Gilbert O'Sullivan influence for those who remember "Alone Again, Naturally!" Album number three continued the folk-pop synthesis, under the direction of a bright young producer by the name of John Pantry, who brought another kind of synthesis—a prototype string synthesizer, giving us access to orchestral sounds at the touch of a keyboard.

There must have been a few extra dollars available for the follow-up album *Breaking of the Dawn* in 1976, because the record company had splashed out on trumpets, trombones, violins, viola, cello, and harp! This time the recording also had—wait for it—an archetypal '70s gatefold sleeve! The material reflected a period of self-discovery, and observations of what made people "tick." Much of it was me being intensely honest and personal, with song titles like "My True Feelings" and "Being Myself in Jesus." The pressures and intensity of life on the road as part of a traveling team was a very effective "refiner's fire" with plenty of trash rising to the surface day by day—good character-building stuff and grist for the songwriter's mill!

Interestingly, there was one track that people would sing along to in concert. "Why Do You Weep?" had a Yiddish feel to it, and in effect became one of my earliest praise songs in a "live" setting. "In Your Way"—another number from the *Breaking of the Dawn* album—crossed over into worship song territory, too.

However, it was the most dramatic track that took pride of place and became a closing number at my gigs. "Peter at the Breaking of the Bread" took the listener from Judas' betrayal, through Peter's denial and finally to Jesus' resurrection. The song would build up a kind of tension until the grand finale at the end, with the triumphant cry "He is alive!"

In concert, I would use the body of my guitar percussively, with various slaps and heartbeat-type sounds that worked well—especially with the lights down low. It was very atmospheric. I often felt the power of the Holy Spirit affirming the proclamation that Jesus is alive, which is basically the same as what happens in worship where you proclaim a truth and you sense God's power in a particular way.

So while I was learning the songwriter's and storyteller's craft—which laid the foundation for my worship composing—I was also learning some of the skills for worship leading, the gospel story leading into a heart response.

Behind the Songs

> Our established English "churchianity" was of a more cerebral variety and suspicious of emotion.... There was an expectation building among many people for an experience of God in the act of worship.

There wasn't usually a sense of drama to worship in the early days. Often it was little more than a sing-along of favorite choruses, a matter of singing out of *Youth Praise* or some other songbook. Songs tended to be about God—not addressed to God. There wasn't the sense of engaging with the Holy Spirit in a special moment. Part of the problem was cultural. Our established English "churchianity" was of a more cerebral variety and suspicious of emotion. But the threshold was in sight. There was an expectation building among many people for an experience of God in the act of worship.

Through events like Spring Harvest, Youth for Christ tours, and the renewal movement that was affecting most denominations, the culture was changing. Many of us felt that in some way God would visit us and we'd experience his presence in a tangible sort of way. That dynamic was one of the main things that drove the development of what we now call "worship leading." There were the beginnings of a sense of adventure—knowing that even if you had your list of songs, the worship could veer off in almost any direction.

Breaking of the Dawn

Behind the Songs

God Put a Fighter in Me
Music from the Crucible of Experience

Fighter

My eyes may see the coming King
in all his majesty, in company all dress'd in white,
but meanwhile here at the world's dark end
the dragon draws the iron curtain round against the light.

    And souls grow weary in this
    war of love, and seek their solace
    strolling down the sweet civilian ways,
    but meanwhile here at the world's dark end
    the nations see no future, waiting for the serpent to strike.

Where have all the Christian soldiers gone?
Where is the resistance?
Will no one be strong?
When will we stand up tall and straight,
rise up and storm the gates?

    How can we fail to get excited,
    the battle is ours, why don't we fight it?
    Battalions of darkness rise above me, but
    God put a fighter in me, put a fighter in me.

So we will sing songs of victory,
we will arise and set them free,
we will applaud your majesty, we will proclaim your kingdom come,
we will announce the battle done, we will lift up the Righteous One.

God Put a Fighter in Me

Listen and you'll hear the sweetest sound
you've ever heard in England,
it's the Spirit blowing across the land,
it's the voice of one who calls his Bride
to come and to be ready,
gentle as a dove
he comes with fire.

>Where have all the Christian soldiers gone?
>Where is the resistance?
>Will no one be strong?
>How can we fail to get excited,
>the battle is ours, why don't we fight it?
>>darkness rise above me, but
>>God put a fighter in me, put a fighter in me.

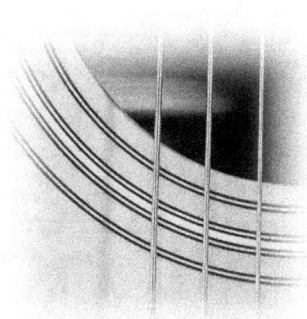

>So we will sing songs of victory,
>we will arise and set them free,
>we will applaud your majesty,
>>we will proclaim your kingdom come,
>>we will announce the battle done,
>>we will lift up the Righteous One.

Copyright © 1979 Kingsway's Thankyou Music

I was incredibly busy—constantly on the road, recently married, and becoming a father for the first time. Jill and I were based in Wolverhampton, the home of British Youth for Christ. And the movement was undergoing a revolution in the late '70s under Clive Calver's leadership. Amid all of that came the *Fighter* album—followed by a 55-date tour that was accompanied by boxes containing thousands of flyers advertising the first of a new annual event called Spring Harvest. We must have been mad.

It was a wacky time. Some crisis might arise having to do with somebody associated with Youth for Christ and I'd get a phone call from Clive. He'd be around in half an hour and we'd be off in the car to the other end of the country troubleshooting. Anything could happen! We needed to learn where to put boundaries in and we hadn't learned that very well. But we were beginning to see how important it is to preserve some time and territory for family and married life.

I'm sure we were very much in a spiritual battle because we were trying to break the mold of how things used to be done and trying to build something new. We may not have seen it in those terms at the time—but I think that was what was happening. We didn't know at the time what Spring Harvest would become, but it was being brought to birth under the leadership of Clive and Pete Meadows, and I was caught up in all of that.

We sensed that we were hitting a spiritual opposition—as well as opposition from people who didn't really want things to change, who were content with how things stood.

As a family we went along to an Anglican church in Wolverhampton. The priest was very supportive of us and I used to meet with him quite often in the mornings and pray. He was very encouraging.

So many things happening, my long absences and a new baby, inevitably put Jill under incredible pressure. Life was a battle. But we were learning a more rugged Christianity, a little bit about endurance and persistence and not giving up. And all that contributed to the song "Fighter."

"Fighter" reflects the fact that I had recognized a particular way in which God was at work in me. The Holy Spirit was urging me on to take action and not to be passive. It was at a time when we were beginning to recognize the importance of a more radical and visionary Christian faith and that's the way that I expressed it in the song, in the context of anticipating Christ's return. I was looking at the state of the world with a kind of battle imagery—a battle for the souls of men and women—and it brings a challenge to the churches: "Where have all the Christian soldiers gone?"

So many things happening, my long absences and a new baby, inevitably put Jill under incredible pressure. Life was a battle.

The accompanying tour was not so much evangelistic as calling Christians toward a more radical commitment. Spring Harvest was coming up as well and we were distributing the flyers. It was all part of the same thing: a search for authentic Christianity, the kind that can change the world. It was a horrendous schedule. But Clive was opening doors for me through his drive and abilities. In turn, I opened doors for him through the music, creating a platform for his preaching.

Long after I'd finished using the song, Sheila Walsh picked up on it, recorded it, and began to use it in concert. I heard her sing "Fighter" at Greenbelt one year with a full band. They gave it an excellent arrangement and their delivery was really powerful. As I listened to it, I felt, "Here's someone else who's taken it to another level and given it a fresh audience." Then Sir Cliff Richard recorded it as well and used it in his concerts when he did his gospel tours.

Behind the Songs

Jesus, Stand Among Us

Jesus, stand among us
    at the meeting of our lives,
        be our sweet agreement
            at the meeting of our eyes.

        O, Jesus, we love you,
            So we gather here,
                Join our hearts in unity
                      And take away our fear.

So to you, we're gathering
    out of each and every land,
        Christ the love between us,
            at the joining of our hands.

        O, Jesus, we love you,
            so we gather here,
                join our hearts in unity
                      and take away our fear.

God Put a Fighter in Me

Jesus stand among us
    at the breaking of the bread,
        join us as one body
           as we worship you, our Head.

        O, Jesus, we love you,
           so we gather here,
                join our hearts in unity
                    and take away our fear.

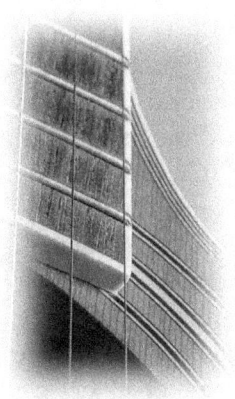

Graham Kendrick
Copyright © 1977 Kingsway's Thankyou Music

> **I invited the kids to silently repeat a line-by-line prayer that I led, and then to speak to us afterwards if they'd prayed it.**
>
> **I didn't have a great deal of faith that anyone would respond.**
>
> **Shame on me!**

Unusually for me, I did an appeal at the end of my concert. I decided to ask for a particular response to what we'd been saying. If they wanted to become Christians, I invited the kids to silently repeat a line-by-line prayer that I led, and then to speak to us afterwards if they'd prayed it. I didn't have a great deal of faith that anyone would respond. Shame on me! We were inundated with more than 30 of these youngsters saying, "I prayed the prayer and I want to be a Christian."

It was part of a church-based mission in Shropshire, so the local Christians were ready to follow up these kids. Years later I was still in touch with the pastor behind the event. He told me that loads of these youngsters are still Christians and still going on with their faith. It was largely that mission that convinced me this was a very effective way of working, compared with one-off events in isolation. When Clive Calver said he wanted to get a team together, I was very keen on the idea.

Being the entrepreneurial type, Clive was the one who had the drive to launch it. He called together prospective members of the team—mostly students he'd worked with in the recent past. Out of that, there were ten of us who committed ourselves to it. It was one of those typically idealistic things that people do when they don't have any experience and don't know any better. But it happens because you believe in it and God is with you. So *In the Name of Jesus* was born.

We had no means of income. I don't know how on earth we thought we were going to get by—or even who would want us. But little by little, through our existing contacts, we eventually had a whole two and a half years of fruitful ministry working with local churches, making loads of mistakes as we went.

One of the biggest challenges with any closely knit team working in a very intense situation is simply being together. What do you do when relationships break down? How do you handle personality clashes? We made every mistake in the book and worked ridiculous hours with no days off—until we started to see the damage it did and learned from our experience.

We pursued the strange ideal of "living by faith." That means you pray the money will arrive just in time! We were constantly slipping "into the red" financially, but somehow kept slipping out again. We believed that God would provide—and he did time and time again—and usually at the last minute. A Christian businessman supplied us with a brand-new estate car. The churches we were working with would also remunerate us as best they could. I was selling a few albums that helped keep me afloat.

When the guy who did the bookkeeping was off sick, I was asked to take on that responsibility for a few weeks. I had no idea. I'd never even heard of the term "cash flow." I paid all the outstanding bills immediately, and then wondered why the account went seriously into the red. There was a sense of relief when the bookkeeper got better.

On another occasion, I had to play the role of mediator between two team members seriously at odds with one another. I was sitting in a van between these two people, trying desperately to resolve their clash. One young guy couldn't take the pressure anymore. Out of sheer frustration he thumped the side of the van so hard it left a dent. I'm just glad he didn't hit me!

God probably did more for us than we did for the churches that we visited.

One of the most productive things about it was working closely with Clive Calver. He and I are total opposites in character and giving—but we balanced each other out.

These days, Clive is a wonderful diplomat. But at the time he was very much the angry young man and aggressive entrepreneur. That mix doesn't always delight other people! I was the calm, quiet, secure, thoughtful, easygoing type. I needed his drive and dynamism. He needed my security and reflective nature. As a result of that partnership we worked together for a period of seven years. I provided the music and he did the sermons.

The excitement and optimism of the late '60s and early '70s was being replaced by the hard reality of life on the road. We were working out our faith with fear, trembling, and tantrums! We were also young and idealistic. And to our dismay, horrendous situations would surface in some of the churches we visited. You'd find yourself sitting in a room with a church leader who'd been indulging in some serious sin. It was a fast-track initiation into some of the more painful realities of church life.

One of the first worship songs I wrote came out of that time. It was called "Jesus Stand Among Us." Church used to mean rubbing shoulders once a week. Suddenly through team ministry, our lives were wrapped up in one another. So the song was an echo of our prayer—"be our sweet agreement at the meeting of our eyes."

I wrote a lot of material in response to what was happening in our lives. Somebody would be going through a particularly difficult time and perhaps I'd write a song as my way of trying to encourage them. We were also doing a lot of counseling, so those special moments of prayer and conversation are probably reflected in songs over the years.

At that time there was very little publishing infrastructure for new praise and worship songs, and songs spread by word of mouth. During a meeting, people would copy the lyrics from the overhead projector and guess the chords as we played. Geoff Shearn was working for Kingsway Music, which was just beginning to publish *Songs of Fellowship*. In the late '70s he discovered that I had a stockpile of these songs, so it was suggested that I record some of them. I dug them out of a drawer and started releasing worship albums alongside the more performance stuff.

I saw it as a sideline. My self-image was quite firmly as a performing artist, and I remember resisting the suggestion of leading worship at the first ever Spring Harvest in 1979! I saw myself singing to people—not leading them in singing. But increasingly I realized that God was doing something new in the area of worship, and many of the skills I'd learned in performing enabled me to serve what was happening. Spring Harvest created a platform and a demand for new songs. A whole generation was expressing itself differently and doing church differently. A new era had begun for me, as well as the Church.

God Put a Fighter in Me

The Blame

The hour is near,
my friends still sleeping,
I am so alone
in this garden
yet all hell and heaven
are watching me.
    If only there could be

    some other way
    than this I'm taking.

I see a valley
of shadow and death
open wide now to swallow me.
    Darkness awaits
    and my soul cries out
    but there will be no comfort.
Father, if you are willing,
take this cup far
from my lips.
    Now that my hour has come
    I see the blame
    falling on me.

Oh watch with me
your eyes so heavy,
it comes so hard
to have to face
this time alone.
    Is that the door
    of heaven I see
    closing hard against me?

Oh such a heavy
load has leapt
upon my shoulders.
    History breathes
    atrocities into my ears,
    drawn from the veins
    of the human race.
I smell the serpent's poison
heaped like the
blackest mountain.
    I see the blame
    falling on me.

God Put a Fighter in Me

My work is done,
the words are spoken,
now like fireflies
the torches dance,
closer through the trees,
casting shadow masks
on the faces of the mob
as they come like a pack of wolves
for me.

    I am betrayed
    by a kiss of a friend
    with a voice so familiar.
Weapons of war for your fear
as if I was a man of violence.
    Future and past so dark
    are crowding in upon this moment,
    but I am ready now
    to see the blame
    falling on me.

Judas, my friend,
how the bag of
thirty silver pieces
weighs so heavy
upon your neck,
and how your eyes
avoid mine;
yes, I'm the Man.
    Why so afraid
    and why the weapons
    and the cloak of darkness?
Let us go now.

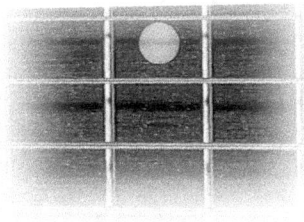

Graham Kendrick
© Copyright Control

I met the Anglican renewal leader David Watson at a Christian festival. I told him I'd had a sense that it was time for me to move on from where I was based in Wolverhampton. He told me about the creative development in music and the arts at St. Michael-le-Belfry Church, and made a few welcoming noises. It was enough to point me in his direction.

Moving to York was an important decision for us. We'd been in five years of an incredible hothouse of activity with both In the Name of Jesus and Youth for Christ, and needed some space to establish ourselves as a family. In moving to another house and another part of the country where people didn't really know who we were, we were able just to be accepted as ourselves.

York is a beautiful place to live. It's an ancient city, dating back to Viking and Roman times. It attracts a lot of tourists, which gives it a holiday atmosphere. We had two more children while we were up there. As far as church was concerned I didn't have any official responsibilities, which meant that we could just enjoy being part of the congregation most of the time.

Despite my Baptist background and Jill's Methodist roots, we had worshipped in a small Anglican church for several years at Wolverhampton, but St. Michael's was a very innovative center with a lot of dance, drama, and music. David Watson had been involved in developing the arts and used to take teams out to do citywide and university missions. It was a stimulating place to be. At the time Graham Cray was the priest, and he kindly agreed to meet with me occasionally, in response to my request for some pastoral accountability.

St. Michael's were pioneers in the Anglican renewal movement, yet still had a bedrock of tradition. That gave me more of an appreciation of liturgy, which began to surface in my songwriting and when I started to write praise marches, which some described as a liturgy for the streets.

Several months into our time in York, I met Geoffrey Stevenson, the very talented mime artist who was at the same church. I invited him to come on a tour that I'd already arranged. He did a number of solo mime pieces and also worked out one or two mimes to accompany songs. It worked so well and produced such a good response that we ended up touring together for about four years. We did lots of events and tours, and worked on two music and mime productions—*Nightwatch* and *The Blame*—which we took to universities and colleges. A prodigiously talented young musician from New Zealand, Chris Norton, also a St. Michael's member, often joined us on the road, providing rich synthesizer backings.

We piled everybody and everything into a box truck—complete with backdrop scenery and lighting. I suppose you could say it was quite "arty"

It was a different thing altogether. There was an element of the theatrical. But we still had to do it on a shoestring! We piled everybody and everything into a box truck—complete with backdrop scenery and lighting. I suppose you could say it was quite "arty"—and it went down well in the venues. We made two albums of the music from the productions, and recorded them economically in a local studio to accompany the tours. The term "low-budget" comes to mind, but there were some quite interesting songs. *The Blame* focused on Jesus taking the blame—the responsibility for the sins of the world—upon himself. The title track centered on the garden of Gethsemane.

The truth contained in that song struck me again on a recent trip to Israel. Our tour guide showed us the way they used to process olives. They would have an olive press consisting of two huge heavy stones that would squeeze out the oil. It brings a whole new meaning to what Jesus went through when you realize that Gethsemane means "olive press." Jesus was placed under incredible pressure with sweat like drops of blood coming from him as he made his choice to go to the cross and take the blame for the sins of the world.

God Put a Fighter in Me

Anywhere You Walk

In the face of a Jew,
    in the eyes of a peasant,
refugee child
    in an age of oppression.

    Creeping 'cross the stateline,
        living on the breadline,
    somehow growing up
        like a flower in the desert.

        Under martial law,
           jackboot justice,
        one of the poor,
           one of the hungry.

           Numbered with the rejects,
              mocked by the elite,
           political dissident,
              man of grief.

God Put a Fighter in Me

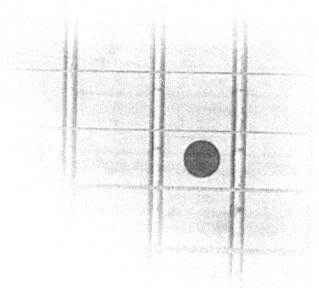

Anywhere you walk,
he's been there before;
anything you feel,
he felt more.

Tried without a lawyer,
accused by liars,
abandoned by justice,
convicted by a riot.

Offered as a scapegoat,
sentenced without evidence,
betrayed by a close friend,
silenced for convenience.

Graham Kendrick
© Copyright Control

Behind the Songs

Bad Company

The Jew and his rabble
keep an appointment with thieves,
cocktails with quislings,
not where the holy should be seen.

Dirt in his fingernails
like a rough working man,
patronized by a few patronizing
aristocrats with lily-white hands.

We'd like you much better
if you would stop keeping that
bad company,
all those social lepers.
We like your ideals
and your street appeal,
it's just the
bad company
embarrassing me.
Da da n da da n da
Da da n da da n da

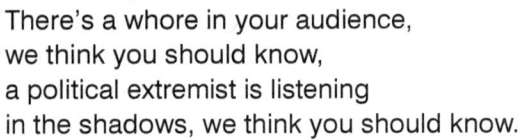

There's a whore in your audience,
we think you should know,
a political extremist is listening
in the shadows, we think you should know.

'Cause your reputation
is being soiled by your dubious friends,
your sympathizers in high places would
respectfully advise you to think again.

God Put a Fighter in Me

            Your hands are dirty
          and our hands are clean;
           our love is discerning
            but your love seems blind
          to the difference between
        the whole and the sick,
      the mad and the sane,
    the poor and the rich,
    the black and the white,
the wrong and the right.

We'd like you much better
if you would stop keeping
that bad company.
All those social lepers,
parasites, communists,
immigrants, terrorists,
bad company.
Impoverished, illiterate,
unhappy, helpless,
bad company
bothering me.
Da da n da da n da
Da da n da da n da

But the Jew and his rabble
keep an appointment with thieves.

Graham Kendrick
© Copyright Control

Behind the Songs

It was the late '70s. News had just broken that Bob Dylan—prophet, poet, and priest of the so-called "protest" movement—had become a born-again, Bible-believing Christian. Not everyone was thrilled about that, of course. His fans were divided between those who vehemently objected, and those who were utterly delighted. Then in 1979 Dylan released a formal, publicstatement in song. It was called *Slow Train Coming*. I hadn't been a Dylan devotee. But I had to admit, it was an absolutely fabulous album.

Dire Straits frontman Mark Knopfler played guitar for Dylan on that recording. That style very much appealed to me. It was gritty and earthy and had some lyrical bite to it. I was looking for a fresh sound and along with several Dire Straits albums, *Slow Train Coming* was a big influence. So we recruited some musicians who could produce a similar sound. And my album *Cresta Run* was the result.

"Anywhere You Walk" was the closing track on side one. It had a reggae-style beat. Lyrically it was an attempt to undermine the cozy picture of a blond-haired, blue-eyed Jesus dressed in a fluorescent robe floating around doing his miracles, and whose feet don't even touch the ground—let alone get dirty. I've always been gripped by the idea of the humanity of Jesus. Without compromising his divinity, he was experiencing the human condition to the maximum.

It was more of what I'd been trying to do for years in these kinds of songs—taking ancient stories and giving them a contemporary context. This is God identifying with all kinds of human conditions, by entering into the experience of them. I wanted the song to help people approach a God who, far from being distant and detached, was totally qualified to give comfort and understanding.

I remember presenting the *Cresta Run* material at Spring Harvest in 1981. It was in the days when the event was held at Prestatyn in North Wales. The crowd had just gulped down their beans on toast or whatever they'd eaten in their cabins, and had braved the strong winds as they rushed to the venue, probably with the intention of snoozing along while Graham Kendrick gently plucked his acoustic guitar.

What they got instead was me and a rock 'n' roll wall of sound coming out of the PA—thanks to some backing tapes! Well, I had warned them that it would be a bit different. But thankfully, there was a positive response. One guy came up to me and, visibly impressed, asked, "So who did you get to play guitar on that?" Tongue firmly in cheek, I said, "Mark Knopfler." Of course, I told the truth before he spread the word round the vacation village!

"Bad Company" was written around the same time, written in a similar vein to "Anywhere You Walk." It was written with the intention of shocking people into a real picture of who Jesus was and who he associated with. He was heavily criticized by the religious authorities of the day because of the company he kept: the Zacchaeuses of the world—the tax collectors regarded as traitors because they collaborated with the Romans; Simon of the Zealots, who were like an underground resistance movement; and the prostitutes and sinners he was constantly seen with.

The words are hammered out like tabloid headlines from the newsstand. It's a very accusatory sort of song, taking the position of the offended establishment and perhaps there's an echo of the anti-establishment attitudes of the times in which it was written. I remember it was always one of those songs you had to use quite carefully because it was meant to be a little bit disturbing, to move people out of their comfort zones.

> **What they got instead was me and a rock "n" roll wall of sound coming out of the PA— thanks to some backing tapes!**

Behind the Songs

Nicodemus

As the watchman's fires burn low, through the curfew streets I go,
the shuttered house stands silent as I whisper through the door "hello,"
Peter turns the key, through an open door I see
a lamplit face at a table place, waiting, so it seems, for me.

I see by your smile you know me well,
you know the score, yes, I am still
a most upstanding citizen respected by them all.
Yes, I've been good, could I do more?
I say my prayers and help the poor,
Holy Moses knows I've kept the rules
but am I alright with you?

How can I who've lived so long, feel so right yet be so wrong,
and now you say I stand outside your kingdom.
But I can't argue or correct you, the words you say I can't reject,
you speak as one whose word cannot be broken.
Tell me, Jesus, what can I do to be right with you,
to be right with you.

And with the shadows closing in, he spoke and touched me deep within,
while soft outside a baby cried and moths danced round the candle flame.
Hey, what's that you're saying, that I must be born again, then my
life appears as wasted years I never did begin.

God Put a Fighter in Me

Sometimes in the lamplight of my room,
I've wished that overnight I could believe in you.
Oh when I am here talking with you, Jesus, anything seems possible,
but to be born again just seems crazy,
you have my respect and more, I'd like to believe in you, I'm trying to,
I need to be right with you, oh I need to be right with you,
and so goodnight, I must be home
before the morning light.

    And when I've made my mind up,
    and when I've made my mind up,
                and when I've made my mind up,
                I'll let you know.

Graham Kendrick
© Copyright Control

Behind the Songs

It's in the middle of the night. There's a certain brooding darkness about the situation—this guy coming secretly at night to see Jesus and then having this extraordinary conversation about being born again. Here was a really upstanding citizen who really kept the rules. But still he wanted to know if he was OK as far as Jesus was concerned. When I looked at the story of Nicodemus, it was those key elements that appealed to me.

Deep down, we all want to know the same answers as Jesus' night visitor. If we're sincere seekers after God, it's the ultimate question: "What do you think of me, God?" There are issues in there to make people think—particularly the whole born-again subject. The resulting song appeared on my *Triumph in the Air* album in 1980.

I've never tired of writing story songs. It's a challenge I enjoy—trying to capture a situation, a biblical story, and retelling it. And it's a worthy task for any Christian involved in the arts—to take ancient truths and bring them alive again for a new generation, without compromising their historical authenticity.

It's often argued that people remember a lyric that's hung on a tune much more than they remember a sermon.

A lot of my songs have been triggered by the preaching and teaching I've heard over the years. There were some great storytellers around in my early years, like Gordon Bailey. He made a big impression on me. He is a very talented communicator and very amusing. He'd have the whole of the audience in the palm of his hand. He's the kind of guy who would retell a Bible story in a tremendously entertaining way, then when he had your attention and your defenses were down, deliver the sting of truth!

In more recent times, my songwriting has been influenced by my association with Roger and Faith Forster and the teaching and emphasis I've received within Ichthus Christian Fellowship. I believe much of the songwriter's role within the Church is to do that—to pick up themes and emphases and interpret them in song. It's often argued that people remember a lyric that's hung on a tune much more than they remember a sermon. So if the song is good and memorable and works, it's a very powerful way of communicating truth.

Behind the Songs

The Servant King

From heaven you came, helpless babe,
entered our world, your glory veiled;
not to be served but to serve,
and give your life that we might live.

There in the garden of tears,
My heavy load he chose to bear:
His heart with sorrow was torn,
"Yet not my will but yours," he said.

*This is our God, the Servant King,
he calls us now to follow him,
to bring our lives as a daily offering
of worship to the Servant King.*

Come, see his hands and his feet,
the scars that speak of sacrifice,
hands that flung stars into space
to cruel nails surrendered.

So let us learn how to serve,
and in our lives enthrone him;
each other's needs to prefer,
for it is Christ we're serving.

Graham Kendrick
Copyright © 1983 Kingsway's Thankyou Music

It's done me good to have written "The Servant King." Whether it's in family life or traveling ministry, there are daily choices to be made in the area of servant attitude. Am I really there to serve God and my brothers and sisters—or to serve my own interests? And it's at that point that I sometimes remind myself I'm the writer of "The Servant King"—so I'd better live it! It's like nailing your colors to the mast. I wish I could claim to have always made the right choice.

The song was written to reflect the theme of Spring Harvest 1984, and contains my most quoted line: "hands that flung stars into space to cruel nails surrendered." I can remember composing it in the little music room at our house in York, where we were living at the time. I wrote it on the piano—despite my severe limitations on that instrument. My colleague Chris Norton helped me make the piano part more presentable.

In a sense it's a little teaching package—with a worship heart to it. At the time I was trying to learn how to serve as a worship leader, a songwriter—and a dad! Our children were small in those days, and as other mothers and fathers will testify, your life is not your own when you are a parent.

As we set out to discover what the Christian life was and how to live it in our generation, servanthood became one of the values we sought to embrace. It's a fundamental principle in ministry that you are there to serve. If you are a worship leader, it can mean that your best way of serving God one particular evening is not to lead. So you just stand in the background while something else happens—because it's not about you. It's about serving God's purposes.

It affects everything we do—including the simple things like what songs do we choose as a worship leader. Do we choose songs just because we like them, or do we choose songs that help that particular group of people to worship God?

It's not an easy choice because there's always such a mixture of people. But if you're into a certain style and yet you find yourself in a church where people find it very difficult to worship in that style, then you have to adapt as much as you can. The point is that you're there to help them give their worship to God. You're not there to perform your worship while they watch. We all have to keep guarding our hearts to try and stay in that place.

The musical style and much of the stagecraft of contemporary praise and worship has been modeled to a significant degree on pop and rock music, which is so much about image, performance, and entertainment. So we have to constantly check that we're not slipping into inappropriate attitudes and values, and that it doesn't become all about what's cool, what's uncool, and what's the latest song—as if it was all about "the charts."

There's a lot of pressure in churches to sing the latest songs. I think the question should always be asked, why this song, why on this occasion? If there is a good reason to and if it's really serving what God's doing in a particular church and if it's really helping people worship, then great. But if an ancient hymn—or a 10-year-old song or a 20-year-old song—does the job better, then use that. It's back to serving again. We are trying to equip the body of Christ to serve the Lord in worship.

We're in a battle with the world, the flesh, and the devil. And worship is going to come under attack. You can look at the whole human race and see there's a battle going on for worship. So where you have music that serves worship, there's going to be a battle over it sooner or later.

Behind the Songs

There's a Sound on the Wind (Battle Song)

There's a sound on the wind like a victory song,
listen now, let it rest on your soul.
It's a song that I learn'd from a heavenly King,
it's the song of a battle royal.

> There's a loud shout of victory that leaps from our hearts
> as we wait for our conquering King.
> There's a triumph resounding from dark ages past
> to the victory song we now sing.

*Come on, heaven's children, the city is in sight,
there will be no sadness on the other side.*

> There'll be crowns for the conquerors and white robes to wear,
> there will be no more sorrow or pain.
> And the battles of earth shall be lost in the sight
> of the glorious Lamb that was slain.

Now the King of the ages approaches the earth,
he will burst through the gates of the sky.
And all men shall bow down to his beautiful name;
we shall rise with a shout, we shall fly!

Graham Kendrick
Copyright © 1978 Kingsway's Thankyou Music

It was a little bit tongue-in-cheek. I'd written "There's a sound on the wind" like an American revivalist-style hymn. I wasn't mocking such music, but I knew I was borrowing a genre that wasn't really mine. I was taking some echoes of the past and bringing them into the present—making a connection with past movements of the Church.

The song was put on the Fighter album. Then a couple of the leaders came up to me at Spring Harvest saying, "You should teach us all that song." I'd never really intended it to be used congregationally. It was an album track. But when we played it, people really responded and loved it—and it became one of the early "standards" at Spring Harvest.

There was certain reluctance on my part to accept the role of worship leader, although the transition was gradual. Firmly fixed in my mind was the image of myself as this singer-songwriter-performer. Becoming a worship leader felt almost like I'd come to an end of something, and I have to confess that I saw the role of worship leader as somewhat second class.

However, when I finally stopped the concert work I suddenly felt liberated. Jill said it was like a burden had lifted from me and I was doing exactly what I should do, as I was so much freer. It was a change of season—you come to the end of something and then go into something new and the overlap between the two can sometimes be an uncomfortable place to be.

In some ways it was a sacrifice for me to contemplate making that step of leaving the singer-songwriter days behind. But once I'd made the transition, it wasn't a sacrifice at all. I just knew it was right to move on, and the songs were beginning to spread around—across the church spectrum.

I was reasonably well known as a singer-songwriter before I was known for worship so that helped to give a neutral platform, too. I was just "Graham Kendrick"—I wasn't "Graham Kendrick representing such and such a denomination or movement." So that allowed my work to be accepted across the church networks and streams. My historic links with cross-denominational organizations like Youth for Christ and Spring Harvest also helped me to access a variety of areas in the global church family.

I'm sure God has given grace for the neutrality of my work. When it comes to gathering people across the divides, worship is the highest common denominator. If you try to gather around secondary matters of doctrine or a particular style of churchmanship, you never get anywhere because there's so much potential disagreement in the detail. But if it's all about the essentials of the Christian faith, a love for God that transcends all those things, and if your message is a call to worship Jesus, then people tend to forget their differences.

People really responded and loved it—and it became one of the early "standards" at Spring Harvest.

Behind the Songs

Carnival of Praise
Taking It to the Streets

Behind the Songs

This Is My Beloved Son

This is my beloved Son
who tasted death
that you, my child, might live.
    See the blood he shed for you,
    what suffering,
    say what more could he give?
        Clothed in his perfection
        bring praise, a fragrant sweet
        garlanded with joy,
            come worship at his feet

        Look, the world's great harvest fields
    are ready now
    and Christ commands us: "Go!"
    Countless souls are dying
so hopelessly,
his wondrous love unknown.
    Lord, give us the nations
for the glory of the King.
Father, send more laborers
the lost to gather in.

Carnival of Praise

That the Lamb who was slain
might receive the reward,
might receive the reward
of his suffering.

Come the day when we will stand
there face to face,

        what joy will fill his eyes.
        For at last his bride appears,
        so beautiful,
        her glory fills the skies.
        Drawn from every nation,
        people, tribe, and tongue;
            all creation sings,
                the wedding has begun.

Graham Kendrick
Copyright © 1985 Kingsway's Thankyou Music

The Moravians experienced a move of God in 1727 that triggered a wave of nonstop intercession lasting 100 years. And of course they continue to be an inspiration for prayer movements like the 24-7 initiative.

I was leading a worship conference with a team in the Czech Republic not far from the home territory of some of these prayer warriors—whom many regard as the mothers and fathers of modern mission. During a break, I took a walk with longtime friend and music director Steve Thompson. We talked about the Christian heritage in that part of Europe, and I mentioned my plans to share one particular story about the Moravians in the evening meeting.

It concerned Leonhard Dober and David Nitschmann, two young men who heard about the terrible plight of slaves on the island of St. Thomas in the West Indies—and how desperately they needed the Gospel. Dober and Nitschmann concluded that the only way for a missionary to reach the slaves there was to become a slave himself, since after working all day on the plantations they were kept by a strict curfew to their huts by night. Only by working alongside them in the sugarcane fields could anyone hope to have a chance

"Let us give to the Lamb the reward for his sufferings"

of sharing the Gospel. This daunting prospect didn't deter them, and some time later they set off for St. Thomas.

In December 1732 their ship came in sight of the island. Ahead of them lay danger, disease, and possible slavery. Yet it was at this moment that Dober is reported to have turned to Nitschmann and, taking one of the mottoes of the Moravian movement, said, "Let us give to the Lamb the reward for his sufferings."

Steve then told me that his father had become a Christian in a Moravian church, on that very same island, founded by those very same missionaries! It was amazing to suddenly find that here was a connection. That evening we introduced Steve as one of their spiritual "grandchildren."

The Moravians' spirit of mission has made quite an impact on Ichthus Christian Fellowship, the church I attend. Ichthus began with just 14 people in Forest Hill in 1974 with a vision to evangelize into the local housing estates. Since then, some 30 congregations have spread across south London, and Ichthus doubles as a missionary-sending agency, with around 80 people (counting children) working in 15 nations.

Leader Roger Forster loves to tell stories about the Moravians. Their community was mostly composed of religious refugees and dissidents who'd been chased out of their countries because of their faith. A benevolent aristocrat with an incredible name—Count Ludvig Nicklaus von

Zinzendorf—gave them sanctuary on one of his estates. From there they began to send missionaries to the ends of the earth. It was a time when you'd have more chance of being shipwrecked than actually reaching your destination.

Their slogan that "the Lamb who was slain might receive the reward of his suffering" drew my attention to how worship and mission really amount to the same thing. From a heart of worship, the Moravians were laying down their lives to take the gospel to the far-flung corners of the earth.

It was definitely a moment of revelation for me. We often talk as if worship and mission are two different things. But surely one of the greatest offerings of worship we can bring is to share the gospel with someone who then becomes a worshipper. The idea is to multiply worshippers. Don't just be a worshipper—bring other worshippers.

It was in the context of hearing Roger's talks that I thought the Moravians' mission statement would make a great chorus to a song. That's how it often works. You hear some teaching and it stirs you and touches your heart. Then you begin to think, "We could be singing that." And of course, much of the power of songs is if we can—by God's grace—capture a message and get people singing it, it gets into our minds and our hearts. That's what I was trying to do with that song.

The Moravians were responsible for sending out more than 3,000 evangelists, taking the gospel to most countries in Europe as well as the Americas, Asia, and Africa. Steve Thompson is not alone in owing a great debt to Moravian missionaries. John Wesley does, too!

Carnival of Praise

Behind the Songs

The Candle Song

Like a candle flame,
flick'ring small
in our darkness.
Uncreated light
shines through infant eyes.

God is with us, alleluia,
God is with us, alleluia.
Come to save us, alleluia,
come to save us, alleluia.
Alleluia.

Stars and angels sing,
yet the earth
sleeps in shadows;
can this tiny spark
set a world on fire?

Yet his light shall shine
from our lives,
Spirit blazing,
as we touch the flame
of his holy fire.

Graham Kendrick
Copyright © 1988 Make Way Music

Behind the Songs

It was a hot summer's day. The sun was streaming in through the windows. Everyone else was enjoying the weather outside. Me? I was locked in "serious songwriter" mode, gently cooking in the heat, and trying to compose Christmas material. It wasn't easy. There was a serious lack of tinsel and turkey.

But I completed the songs, and proceeded to another sunless place—the recording studio—to meet the deadlines for an autumn release. So by the time Christmas came, I'd had enough of Christmas!

The Gift was a festive presentation for outreach events in shopping centers. We issued an instruction book full of resource ideas to help churches make use of the presentation, and encouraged them to give out invitations to Christmas carol services and so on. From all the reports we got, it worked very well and is still very popular. It included a song called "Peace to You," which was designed to be sung to passersby as a blessing.

"The Candle Song" was part of it, too. It was also the first time I had ever recorded a boy choir. Of all the songs I included in *The Gift*, it's probably the one that carries the most echoes of traditional Christmas music. The central image is of the candle flame, a symbol of this vulnerable little child coming into the world. How amazing that God should take that kind of risk.

I was trying to interest an American publisher in some of my festive material. And they told me, "There are 27 Christmas songs. That's it. You re-package the 27, or whichever of the 27 you want to." Like it or not, there's actually a lot of truth in that, because much of what people want is the nostalgia, the memories of childhood Christmases, and so on. Of course, with increasing secularization, the nostalgic connections are shifting to nonreligious seasonal songs—like George Michael's "Last Christmas."

But even so, the Christian Christmas traditions are a great foundation on which to build. For me—and I think for any Christian writer—the challenge is to go beyond the trappings and unpack what was really going on then, and what it means for a person living today.

I was trying to do the same in "Once Upon a Universe," one of the songs from the *Millennium Chorus*. I wanted to say something about the incarnation in a nonreligious way, so that as you listen to that track, you wouldn't necessarily think, "Oh this is a Christmas song." There are no sleigh bells, but it tries to tell the story: "Once upon a universe underneath these same stars, the most amazing thing happened...."

The God who sent the galaxies cartwheeling into space, set the planets spinning, put the moon and stars in place, was born, and now God has cried children's tears." I hope someone out there will suddenly sit up and think, "Wow, could that baby really have been God?"

He didn't send a host of angels or some alien spaceship to rescue us all.

He sent a baby, in a society with a high infant mortality rate and despots like Herod, who were willing to kill babies to protect their own interests.

People have vague recollections of Christmas being something about God showing his love to us. Yet the incarnation is a totally stunning, mind-blowing thought. If the creator truly became a human being, then that moment has to be the defining moment not only of human history, but the defining moment of the whole universe.

He didn't send a host of angels or some alien spaceship to rescue us all. He sent a baby, in a society with a high infant mortality rate and despots like Herod, who were willing to kill babies to protect their own interests.

If you want to know what the universe means, then you have to look at the life that was lived by the creator of that universe who was made flesh.

Carnival of Praise

Behind the Songs

Earth Lies Spellbound

Earth
is spellbound in darkness,
sin's oppressive night;
yet in Bethlehem
hope is burning bright.
Mysteries are unfolding,
but the only sign
is a manger bed
where a baby cries.

Crowding stairways of starlight,
choirs of angels sing:
"Glory, glory to God
in the highest heaven."
Peace is stilling the violence,
hope is rising high,
God is watching us now
through a baby's eyes.

Wake up! Wake up! It's Christmas morning,
Christ's eternal day is dawning.
Angels sing in exultation,
fill the streets with celebration.
Now to God on high be glory,
to the earth proclaim the story.
Ring the bells in jubilation,
tell the news to every nation:
Christ has come!

Weakness shatters the powerful,
meekness shames the proud,
vain imaginings
come tumbling down.
Ancient mercies remembered,
hungry satisfied,
lowly, humble hearts
are lifted high.

Graham Kendrick
Copyright © 1994 Make Way Music

Behind the Songs

Out there on the concert circuit, hot on the heels of The Pretenders and The Hollies, and just before the pantomime season, came...Graham Kendrick and *Rumours of Angels*! This was a Christmas presentation aimed at large theaters and concert halls. Our aim was to deliver something of high quality, as good as any other professional show you might attend. It was good to be on the road following the secular tours—and getting a bigger crowd in some cases. But the greatest satisfaction in it all was when local Christians really took a hold of it as an event to bring along friends who wouldn't be seen dead in a church.

Plymouth in particular was an outstanding occasion. One of the church leaders down there, Ian Coffey, who is a friend of mine, had been working with other leaders on a whole program of outreach meetings. They invited us to come down with *Rumours of Angels* as a way of launching this. They'd enlisted the support of over 60 churches and had made it a serious focus for prayer. They ended up packing out the city hall with over 3,000 people—and had to put on a matinee in the afternoon because of the demand. There was such a tremendous atmosphere of God's presence, which you knew was a result of all the prayer. It was one of those days when everything comes together in just the way you dreamed it might.

That's where these events work the best—when you are partnering with the local churches and then making use of it in an ongoing program. We launched it at the NEC in 1994. We did just a couple of other events that first year, then the following year we toured it around several 2,000-seat venues. We recruited local choirs to take part and I took my band. We also had a very talented computer animator who put together some material that accompanied the songs. So the music was synchronized with background material projected onto the screens, which just added to the overall visual impact of the event.

I was conscious that I was revisiting some of the early singer-songwriter territory. It was one of the first things I'd done for the best part of ten years that involved writing some "performance" songs like "Thorns in the Straw"—as well as pieces that were for a soloist or choir as opposed to congregational praise and worship. It was satisfying to see some of the worship elements incorporated into the performance songwriting and vice versa.

It was good to be on the road following the secular tours—and getting a bigger crowd in some cases.

"Earth Lies Spellbound" was another of the songs from the presentation. An attempt at a contemporary carol, it was inspired by the Magnificat—Mary's response to God—as well as passages in Isaiah. One of the battles the songwriter and worship leader fights at Christmas is the weight of nostalgia, sentiment, and tradition, which largely obscures what the story was really all about. But if you look at the Magnificat, Mary's song of praise after being chosen to be the mother of the Son of God, it is a remarkable collection of thoughts about the proud being brought down and the humble lifted high, the hungry being satisfied and so on—things often neglected amid the usual nativity scene narrative.

So the idea was to recapture what the Christmas season is all about, but in such a way that all the resonances are there with the Christmas we know. You have to start where people are—but then take them somewhere they haven't been. There are many Christmas carols that are wonderfully rich theologically. But familiarity breeds contempt and many people sing those songs without the faintest idea what they're actually about. Yet such hymns remain irreplaceable. But in a touring production like *Rumours of Angels*—which did include some traditional material—we were wanting to give people a fresh look at what the incarnation is all about.

There is some beautiful poetry built into the truths of the incarnation. And as a lyricist, I see my job as seeking out

...as a lyricist, I see my job as seeking out the poetry of truth. It's already there. You can't create it. But you can look for it.

the poetry of truth. It's already there. You can't create it. But you can look for it. One of the lines I put into "Earth Lies Spellbound" is: "God is watching us now through a baby's eyes." I was very intrigued with that idea. And when you start to imagine a baby's view of the world, and God watching us, as it were, through a baby's eyes—it's very challenging, especially if the baby in mind is unwanted, or dying from lack of medicine, or treated cruelly.

Behind the Songs

Let the Flame Burn Brighter (We'll Walk the Land)

We'll walk the land with hearts on fire;
and every step will be a prayer.
Hope is rising, new day dawning;
sound of singing fills the air.

Two thousand years, and still the flame
is burning bright across the land.
Hearts are waiting, longing, aching,
for awakening once again.

Let the flame burn brighter
in the heart of the darkness,
turning night to glorious day.
Let the song grow louder,
as our love grows stronger;
let it shine!
Let it shine!

We'll walk for truth, speak out for love;
in Jesus' name we shall be strong,
to lift the fallen, to save the children,
to fill the nation with your song.

Graham Kendrick
Copyright © 1989 Make Way Music

Behind the Songs

It only took us an hour to fly up to Edinburgh. And we knew it was going to take us three weeks to walk all the way back! Looking out of the window, we faced the stark reality of what we'd let ourselves in for. None of us had done anything quite like it before. We'd all done some basic physical fitness preparation, but whether we could walk an average of 24 miles a day for 21 days and pray eight hours a day was unknown. Yet we did!

"We'll Walk the Land" was a conscious attempt to write a theme song for the 1989 March for Jesus, when not only praise marches were happening all over the place but also something that came to be known as "prayer walking" was being pioneered. Such activity can best be summed up as "praying on site with insight." It's simply praying in the very places where we expect our prayers to be answered. Walking helps sensitize us to the realities of our communities as we pray.

With others, I shared a vision for not only localized prayer and praise marches but also to actually walk and pray for the whole country. Along with other folks—and in cooperation with something called the Youth with a Mission Torch Run initiative—a scheme was hatched to walk the length of the UK. The following year we walked west to east across the land as well, which, putting the two journeys together, symbolically formed the shape of the cross.

We were walking 20 to 25 miles a day, which produced the most enormous blisters.

I walked the section from Edinburgh to London over a three-week period, with a small team. There was another team that walked from John o' Groats to Edinburgh and a third covered Land's End to London, and we coincided at the March for Jesus that year in the capital. The Edinburgh-to-London section was well over 400 miles because we didn't go in a straight line. We were detouring all over the place, hosted by churches along the way. We were walking 20 to 25 miles a day, which produced the most enormous blisters. And we were praying constantly for the places we were going through, as well as for the UK in general.

When you step out like that (literally for us!), your vision is regularly filled with things to pray about. We were seeing the land and the people—and praying as we went. What you see as you go along praying sometimes takes on symbolic significance. For example, you become aware of the national infrastructure such as the National Grid. We saw these great power cables snaking across the country, and started praying for networks of prayer and relationships to be made across the UK.

Living life at walking pace changes your perspective of the world. I remember walking all day through the countryside and then suddenly finding ourselves crossing an automobile bridge. I looked down at the madness below—vehicles rushing here and there in this incredible hurry—and I thought, "This is crazy. What's motivating everybody to do this, to live like this?" I remember imagining what might be driving each driver, and praying all the harder for people to discover what they had really been created for.

We slept in motorhomes. We'd park for the night on campsites, sometimes on church premises. There was a little bit of media coverage here and there, as local journalists left their desks to ask what on earth were we doing! We would try to contact local churches in the towns on our route. So sometimes people would meet us and walk with us for several hours and then go home. People seemed to find that very encouraging—that others should care enough to walk through their town and pray.

Following a vision shared by Steve Clifford from the Pioneer network of churches, we encouraged people around Britain to march in their regions. Under the banner of "March for Jesus Where You Live," I think there were somewhere around 250,000 involved in about 700 March for Jesus events. So

> **I think there were somewhere around 250,000 involved in about 700 March for Jesus events. So it had hit a pretty massive scale.**

it had hit a pretty massive scale. There was also a sense of breaking fresh ground for this thing called "prayer walking."

Subsequent to that, others have done long-distance prayer walks—people like John Presdee, who walked right through to Istanbul. And then others have joined Lynn Green from Youth with a Mission on the Reconciliation Walk down the old Crusades routes to apologize to the Muslims and Jews for the way they were treated in the name of Christ.

Of course the very concept of walking and praying did not come from just these initiatives. It's one of those things whose origins are difficult to trace, which I always find encouraging. It gives me a bit more evidence that God is behind it. But it has become a regular part of the prayer life of the churches around the world. It's not uncommon to find people talking about going "prayer walking" through their town or around their neighborhood.

We recorded "We'll Walk the Land" at Abbey Road. A Christian record producer who was using the legendary studios in London used some of his "downtime" to record the track as a single. It was my first visit to Abbey Road, where the Beatles recorded so many of their hit songs.

Behind the Songs

> **We invited lots of Christian artists—like Dave Bilbrough, Noel Richards, and Sue Rinaldi—and formed a kind of "Feed the World"-style choir.**

However, the intention behind recording the single wasn't about Graham Kendrick trying to make it into the charts. We really wanted a way of explaining ourselves as March for Jesus, and one of the best ways to do that is through a song. We invited lots of Christian artists—like Dave Bilbrough, Noel Richards, and Sue Rinaldi—and formed a kind of "Feed the World"-style choir.

The song reached the dizzy heights of number 55 in the singles chart! So it wasn't enough to secure airplay. But funnily enough, when so many hit songs of the day quickly faded from memory, "We'll Walk the Land" wasn't forgotten at all. It went on to be sung all over the world.

The lyrics contained phrases like "hope is rising" and "new day dawning"—reflecting the feeling that a new era was beginning. There was a sense of rising hope and expectation in being caught up with things like March for Jesus and other large-scale prayer initiatives—like the Pray for Revival event that drew 15,000 to the NEC in Birmingham.

March for Jesus put us in contact with groups of active Christians in pretty much every nation of the world. We tried hard to give marchers a perspective on their brothers and sisters elsewhere: the churches that are struggling; the churches that are heavily persecuted; as well as the awesome gatherings in South America and Korea. From very tiny gatherings to 2.2 million people in São Paulo and a million-strong prayer gathering in Seoul, March for Jesus was a big eye-opener to us all. Those things spread hope, knowing that Christianity is growing at an incredible rate in some parts of the world.

I've always found that the most effective way to convey the vision behind March for Jesus has been to play video clips of marches from across the globe. Even the toughest-looking church leaders shed a few tears at the sight of so many different tribes and tongues worshipping Jesus.

Behind the Songs

We Believe

We believe in God the Father,
maker of the universe,
and in Christ his Son our Savior,
come to us by virgin birth.
We believe he died to save us,
bore our sins, was crucified.
Then from death he rose victorious,
ascended to the Father's side.

Jesus, Lord of all, Lord of all; Jesus, Lord of all, Lord of all.
Jesus, Lord of all, Lord of all; Jesus, Lord of all, Lord of all.
Name above all names. Name above all names.

We believe he sends his Spirit,
on his Church with gifts of power.
God his word of truth affirming,
sends us to the nations now.
He will come again in glory,
judge the living and the dead.
Every knee shall bow before him,
then must every tongue confess.

Graham Kendrick
Copyright © 1986 Kingsway's Thankyou Music

I grabbed an acoustic guitar and a group of us piled into a minibus. One guy had a bass drum that took up most of the space, but it turned out to be one of the most useful instruments on the day. Guitar strings broke, violins went wildly out of tune, voices grew hoarse—but that drumbeat kept us glued together and carried above the traffic noise. It was one of the embryonic praise marches, when I joined a crowd of folks from my own church and Youth with a Mission.

In the course of establishing a church in Soho, they had decided to pray and worship publicly around the area. Despite my natural reticence at such overt expressions of faith, I had become intrigued with the idea of taking praise out of the four walls of the church and onto the streets. So, resisting the temptation of a relaxing Saturday night at home—a rare treat, as I'd normally be at a worship celebration somewhere—I thought I had better experience it.

It was in the midst of trying to lead one of the groups in prayer and worship through the streets that I perceived the need for a set of songs and prayers that really suited that situation. We were singing songs from our current "indoor" repertoire that were lively and so on. But in many cases I'd get halfway through a song and think, "Well, the first bit was appropriate but now this bit isn't; the chorus is great but the verses just don't fit this situation." One of the very obvious needs was for a simple proclamation of the basics of the Christian faith, such as those encapsulated in the creeds.

> **Guitar strings broke, violins went wildly out of tune, voices grew hoarse—but that drumbeat kept us glued together.**

I took one of the well-known creeds as a starting point, and developed the song "We Believe." I gave it a walking rhythm by walking up and down my room at home, simulating the dynamics of the street procession. It became part of the first praise march I published, but then people began to pick it up for general use. I heard comments about how good it was to have a new credal song that expressed some of the basic content of the Christian faith. More by accident than design, it filled a hole in the worship of charismatic churches, some of whom were realizing that they'd thrown the credal baby out with the liturgical bathwater. And it gave liturgical churches a new rhythmic approach to something very familiar.

I also took the simple proclamation from the liturgy "Christ has died, Christ is risen, Christ will come again," put a bass drum beat behind it, and made it into a rhythmic chant. Again that suited the streets. Rather than just mumbling those simple but powerful truths—as is often the case—it became a confident proclamation.

Psalm 24 seemed appropriate on the streets, having originated as one of the songs of ascent chanted by worshippers approaching the gates of Jerusalem on their way to the temple: "Lift up your heads, O you gates; be lifted up, you ancient doors, that the King of glory may come in." Out on the streets, it became an announcement of Christ's kingdom to the city.

Those who didn't have a liturgical tradition may have had to overcome a little bit of prejudice. But generally people were able to accept it—especially once they took part. The marches did expose non-liturgical people to a kind of liturgy and often that would work back to their churches and their services. It does bring up a general point about the strengths and weaknesses of contemporary praise and worship music, and I think there is a growing concern about content. The potential that songs have of inculcating truth and doctrine to us is not being fully realized.

Having been brought up in a church where the preaching of the word was very central, morning and evening, I learned to value and respect it highly. I can also remember it being impressed upon me, in various ways, so that we had to be very accurate when dealing with

> **I must confess to more than a few blunders. One was in the line "later on the tide came in and washed my nets away." I had overlooked the fact that there is no tide on Galilee because it's an inland sea!**

the Word of God. As a child, I was made to do something called the Scripture Exam at Sunday school—as if there weren't enough exams already—and it mostly consisted of learning certain scriptures word for word. You had to get the punctuation exact as well. Every comma and quotation was marked. I think things like that impressed upon me a great respect for the Word of God. As my songwriting developed, the concern for accuracy was assumed.

However, I must confess to more than a few blunders. A long time after I'd recorded *Footsteps on the Sea*, someone pointed out a couple of inaccuracies in the track "Simon's Song." One was in the line "later on the tide came in and washed my nets away." I had overlooked the fact that there is no tide on Galilee because it's an inland sea!

Behind the Songs

Carnival of Praise

Lord, Have Mercy on Us

Lord, have mercy on us,
come and heal our land.
Cleanse with your fire,
heal with your touch.
Humbly we bow and call upon you now.
O Lord, have mercy on us.

Graham Kendrick
Copyright © 1986 Kingsway's Thankyou Music

Behind the Songs

Greg was standing outside the Odeon Cinema in Leicester Square with his girlfriend and a group of other friends. They were quietly minding their own business when suddenly the air was filled with a strange noise. The routine "buzz" of London's social life was broken momentarily by a crowd of "happy-clappy people," as Greg described them. He immediately realized that this weird bunch were Christians. "My friends and particularly my girlfriend mocked them," he recalled, "but I remember thinking at the time, I really should be with them."

Three years previously, Greg had met some Christians and received prayer. But he didn't stick with it. Faith had faded from his life. However, seeing the praise marchers strut their stuff through Leicester Square made a big impact on him. Eventually the encounter led to his recommitting himself to God. "It was one of those significant points at which God broke into my life," said Greg, "and was a major part in the process of him leading me back to himself."

I'd just happened to ask Greg how he became a Christian. I had no idea he was going to tell me how his life had been transformed by our own experimental praise marches through London several years before, in 1985. Those early excursions into the whole realm of "street praise" sometimes felt embarrassing and clumsy, yet I could not escape the feeling that God was up to something.

Even amid our improvised disorder of those early attempts, I felt we were venturing into something significant. I had a growing conviction that if we were to achieve a significant breakthrough for the kingdom of God in our nation, one of the things we had to do much more was to take praise and worship into the public arena.

> **Those early excursions into the whole realm of "street praise" sometimes felt embarrassing and clumsy, yet I could not escape the feeling that God was up to something.**

Churches all over the country had come into a fresh experience of God in their worship. For the first time in a long time, people were actually enjoying the whole experience of praising God. For many churches, hymn-singing had become a kind of humble duty. Now there was expectation and anticipation when we gathered to worship. But I had some nagging concerns. Were we in danger of becoming inward looking? How could we share Christ with the wider world? How could we help them taste something of this refreshing presence of God?

I also felt that people needed to be reintroduced to the Church as a joyful, caring community—full of life and color. Satan's kingdom needed to be confronted and invaded with the truth of Christ's victory—spoken or sung out with faith and power. It was a tall order to encapsulate all that in a few songs!

To help give some direction and format to that raw boldness of praising God out in the community, I started writing a program of scriptures, songs, and shouts. One of the dynamics of that is the idea of agreement. It crystallizes the prayers of a whole company of people in one moment.

I looked at Anglican liturgy, and also observed how street demonstrations work. I developed a kind of "liturgy for the streets," setting prayer, praise, and proclamation to music. Actually, there was nothing new about it. Movements like the Salvation Army had led the way in taking God's kingdom into the open air with music and proclamation.

The idea took off, and we heard of other "Make Way" marches being held around the country.

The result was the very first recording in that genre, called *Make Way! A Carnival of Praise*. "Lord, Have Mercy on Us" was one of no fewer than 16 songs that were included on the album. It's a straightforward prayer song. There were songs of preparation as well as songs for a praise procession or open-air celebration. A number of songs from that album went on to become established, such as "Meekness and Majesty" and "We Believe."

On the album cover was a photograph of one of the early praise marches we did with Ichthus Christian Fellowship. People had dressed colorfully and made bright banners to wave about as they walked along—some folks were made up as clowns to really convey a fun, carnival atmosphere. The idea took off, and we heard of other "Make Way" marches being held around the country. I opened up an old filing cabinet recently (with a hammer and chisel because we'd lost the key!) and discovered big files of reports from those early events. The initiative itself made way for something on a much grander scale—March for Jesus.

Meekness and Majesty

Meekness and majesty,
manhood and deity,
    in perfect harmony,
    the Man who is God.
Lord of eternity
dwells in humanity,
    kneels in humility
    and washes our feet.

O what a mystery,
meekness and majesty.
Bow down and worship
for this is your God,
this is your God.

Father's pure radiance,
perfect in innocence,
    yet learns obedience
    to death on a cross.
Suffering to give us life,
conquering through sacrifice,
    and as they crucify
    prays: "Father forgive."

Wisdom unsearchable,
God the invisible,
    love indestructible
      in frailty appears.
Lord of infinity,
stooping so tenderly,
    lifts our humanity
      to the heights of his throne.

Graham Kendrick
Copyright © 1986 Kingsway's Thankyou Music

"Meekness and Majesty" was originally written around the theme for yet another Spring Harvest Easter event, but was first recorded on the first praise march album, *Carnival of Praise,* to help prepare people to march in the same manner as their king would march. It's a good example of truth and poetry come together. I remember getting toward the end of the third verse of this song and wondering how to end it. In a song like this you are trying to set a flow of ideas that bring the reader to as much of a conclusion as possible. Then I considered how the incarnation opened the way for the ascension—Jesus returning to his Father's side, and how his plan was to lift us up to share his glory and reign with him forever. So the song concludes, "stooping so tenderly, lifts our humanity to the heights of his throne."

Once I had revisited the truth, it gave me the poetic shape as well. You start with Jesus, Lord of eternity, kneeling in humility and washing our feet. And now having come down to us, he's done all that's necessary so he can take us back up. So he goes back to heaven, taking his humanity with him and all those who have believed in him.

> **Sometimes I will let songs mature a bit before using them outside my own church.**
>
> **They are very patient and have got quite used to me doing that!**

I often approach lyric writing like I imagine a sculptor might take a choice block of marble and look at the veins of the rock, believing there's a beautiful statue in there waiting to be chipped out. The more I chip away, the more I'm going to find some great truths—if only I can chip them out without knocking the nose or ears off by mistake!

Sometimes I will let songs mature a bit before using them outside my own church. They are very patient and have got quite used to me doing that! The song might reappear a few months or weeks later in a slightly different form. Then I have to cope with people saying, "Oh I liked it better the first way!" But it's worth doing for the sake of what you learn. In preparation for a recording project, I often call together a volunteer choir, which helps me road test the songs. Sometimes you are just learning that something is technically difficult. For example, syncopation, which might be second nature to a musician or singer, can be quite problematic to a crowd.

Most useful of all is to see people expressing their worship through the embryonic song, then you know it works.

Probably my greatest regret in songwriting is going too soon with a song without being perfectly sure that I've gone as far as I can in digging out the truth or crafting the melody. It's such a loss if it doesn't quite get there. It could represent countless hours of work.

I was brought up under my father's expositional teaching. So the kind of teaching I heard as a teenager was always very biblical—and it was terribly important to be accurate. When we did the scripture exam at school, everything was marked—including the punctuation being in the right place. That made us think, you mustn't mess with this, this is the Word of God. So all that impressed on me the importance of getting it right, of trying to grasp the truth. And that's carried over into my songwriting.

> **Most useful of all is to see people expressing their worship through the embryonic song, then you know it works.**

There is poetry in truth. If you dig into a truth it will unlock poetry. So a song like "Meekness and Majesty" is very much the poetry of those extremes of the meekness and majesty of God—how can the creator of the earth make himself so small and become a servant of his own creatures? When you start to unpack that, it's endless.

The great Christian leader and author A. W. Tozer wrote in one of his books that he hoped one day somebody would write a song about the meekness and majesty of God because it was such a wonderful theme to him. I think it was after writing the song that I came back to that and thought, "Oh wow, perhaps his prayer has been answered to some degree."

Behind the Songs

O Lord, the Clouds are Gathering

O Lord, the clouds are gathering,
the fire of judgment burns,
how we have fallen!
O Lord, you stand appalled to see
your laws of love so scorned
and lives so broken.

Have mercy, Lord,
forgive us, Lord,
restore us, Lord, revive your church again.
Let justice flow
like rivers
and righteousness like a never-failing stream.

O Lord, over the nations now,
where is the dove of peace?
Her wings are broken.
O Lord, while precious children starve,
the tools of war increase;
their bread is stolen.

O Lord, dark powers are poised to flood
our streets with hate and fear;
we must awaken!
O Lord, let love reclaim the lives
that sin would sweep away,
and let your kingdom come.

Yet, O Lord, your glorious cross shall tower
triumphant in this land,
evil confounding.
Through the fire your suffering church displays
the glories of her Christ:
praises resounding.

Graham Kendrick
Copyright © 1987 Make Way Music

Football hooliganism. Street riots. Teenage single mums. Abortion. Poverty. Child abuse. People were talking about the state of the nation. They were concerned about what was happening to the country, and had a sense of Britain being under God's judgment, having forsaken its Christian heritage. That was the general feeling at a leaders' conference I was attending. And it inspired me to write "O Lord, the Clouds Are Gathering."

It's both a lament and a prayer song. The prayer side of it is based on Amos 5: "Let justice flow like rivers and righteousness like a never-failing stream." That's where it came from. I took notes and later began to turn it into this song.

It's quite unusual for a praise song to start with a line like "O Lord, the clouds are gathering." Budding composers are usually taught at songwriters' workshops to start their pieces with a positive-sounding first line. I'm afraid I went against the flow there. Perhaps the song would have been more popular if I'd given it that kind of intro, but then it was always intended to be a lament leading into prayer. It may not be the sort of song you would choose to start a meeting. However, churches that are in touch with the problems that surround them and have concern for their community would find it very suitable for their prayer meetings.

Part of the challenge in writing it was to draw attention to some of the problems surrounding us without being grotesque on the one hand or sentimental on the other. Visual imagery is a powerful thing. If you can press those buttons and use people's imaginations to do the work for you, and do it succinctly, it helps people to pray in a way that is rooted in the real world, hence lines like: "while precious children starve, the tools of war incease."

There is a call and response in the chorus for the male and female sections of the congregation: "Have mercy, Lord (Have mercy, Lord)." I was definitely going through a phase around that time of doing a lot of that. People were exploring antiphonal songs where you interacted with one another, but in such a way that it wasn't complicated. You didn't have to be a trained choir to do it—it was just another dynamic for an average crowd of people. It was also very suitable for the praise marches because it created another variation within the desired crowd dynamic.

It found a place in such events as the Pray for Revival rallies at the NEC,

Football hooliganism.
Street riots.
Teenage single mums.
Abortion.
Poverty.
Child abuse.

People were talking about the state of the nation.

Birmingham, and proved ideal for a gathering whose specific purpose was to pray for the nation. When people went home they took it with them and began to use it in their prayer meetings and so on. So it's a tool for prayer.

It is appropriate that so many of our songs are bright and joyful. But it would be wrong if we didn't include lament. Where you live in the world is a significant factor, too. Another

Behind the Songs

...you only really enjoy freedom where there is a structure. Form and freedom go together.

composition of mine in that vein was "Who Can Sound the Depths of Sorrow." That was commissioned by Care for the Family for a pro-life context in 1988, but I deliberately made the song a bit more generic, addressing the way in which we treat children in general.

I was pleased I did. Several years ago a church leader from Sri Lanka was passing through our church and thanked me very warmly for the song, adding that it was well used in their country. That surprised me initially because it takes such a serious theme. But he explained that when you live in the context of civil war—witnessing families being torn apart and children murdered in the crossfire—you can't very easily sing bright, happy, celebration songs all the time. You need songs that address what is happening in people's lives—even if it's painful.

We have to be honest. We're not very good at doing that in England. We like to press on with the happy songs because we feel they lift people up and point their hearts toward God. But as well as being extraordinary in joy—as Psalm 45 describes him—Jesus is also a man of sorrows and acquainted with grief. He is supremely qualified to meet us in our griefs and sorrows. The key is in how songs are used. It's the leadership and the pastoral skills that are needed to bring in the right song at the right time.

Sometimes when you need to use a serious song, you have to take the people to the place where they really can engage with it. It may take you most of the meeting to get people from the preoccupation of the cares of daily life into a place where they can intercede or take on a more serious theme.

The high church has requiems. Often that kind of focus is lacking in the supposedly "renewed" churches. We don't seem to have a context for expressing corporate grief. But there are times when it's right to sing out one's sorrow. You have to find the balance. There has to be light as well as shadow, and so a song like "O Lord, the Clouds Are Gathering" can conclude with hope amid the darkness—with the anticipation that God is going to make things right in the end.

I believe there's something here that those leaning toward the spontaneous approach to worship can learn from the liturgical wing of the Church. There is a value in formality, even though large sections of the Church are currently reflecting the world's culture of informality. What the great requiems do is give a guided framework for thoughts and emotions at a certain time, to cope in a certain situation, and they take you on a journey.

It's great if people have the skill to take a congregation, in a spontaneous way, on a journey of thought and emotion. But where those skills don't exist—and even when they do exist—a well-thought-out liturgical journey can be of great value. In any case, you only really enjoy freedom where there is a structure. Form and freedom go together. You can't appreciate liberty without law.

There is evidence of a trend toward a rediscovery of structure in worship. That's very timely because trying to produce the spontaneous, meeting after meeting, can be exhausting. In any case, by definition you can't make the spontaneous happen when you want it to! You can drift into unreality, and everything can become so homespun and anecdotal that you completely lose clarity of doctrine, theology, and good content. Things can become very, very subjective.

Behind the Songs

Rejoice! Rejoice!

*Rejoice! Rejoice! Christ is in you,
the hope of glory in our hearts.
He lives! He lives! His breath is in you,
arise a mighty army, we arise.*

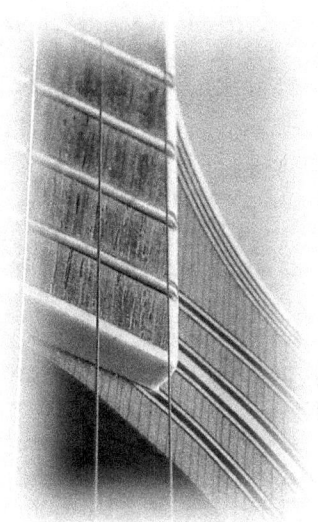

Now is the time for us
to march upon the land;
into our hands
he will give the ground we claim.
He rides in majesty
to lead us into victory;
the world shall see that
Christ is Lord!

God is at work in us
his purpose to perform,
building a kingdom
of power not of words,
where things impossible
by faith shall be made possible;
let's give the glory
to him now.

Carnival of Praise

Though we are weak, his grace
is everything we need;
we're made of clay
but this treasure is within.
He turns our weaknesses
into his opportunities,
so that the glory
goes to him.

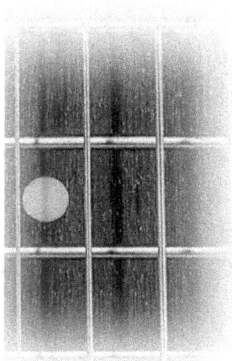

Graham Kendrick
Copyright © 1983 Kingsway's Thankyou Music

Men and women were taking to the streets, surrounding government buildings and military bases around the world—and making an impact. It was the decade of Greenham Common and the miners' strike. It was a time when masses of ordinary people at the grassroots actually got out there and made a difference. It was an explosion of "people power." So it was quite apt that a song should come along in the '80s boasting the line, "Now is the time for us to march upon the land!"

Looking at "Rejoice! Rejoice!" now, you'd think it was all about March for Jesus. But actually it was written two or three years before that came to birth. So at the time of writing I didn't have a specific vision of the street processions that became March for Jesus. It was simply an exhortation and a metaphor to get out there—for the Church to rise up and fulfill its destiny. The track appeared first on my third worship album *Let God Arise*, but reappeared on *Make Way! A Carnival of Praise*, where the marching metaphor became literal.

I recall being inspired by the need to joyfully celebrate the reality of Christ living in us through the Holy Spirit, as a contrast to the tendency toward morbid introspection that I had encountered. Hence, hope-filled lines such as: "where things impossible by faith shall be made possible...though we are weak, his grace is everything we need."

I faced occasional criticism for mentioning "victory" and "triumph" in my songs around this time. Indeed there is danger in triumphalism, and overuse of militaristic imagery can be insensitive and open to misunderstanding by those who might take it literally!

But at the time when these kinds of songs were being widely written, there was a need for the Church to wake up and be more active—and to believe that God can actually do things that will affect our neighborhoods, our towns, and the nations.

There was a need to be more confident and to be a little stronger in the face of evil, unbelief, and the problems that face us. When these emphases first come up they can fill everyone's focus and vision for a while, and the pendulum can swing too far. I hope the balance lay in lines like, "we're made of clay but this treasure is within." It's not that we are great, but that the grace and mercy of God is great and well worth shouting about—there has to be a humility that faces up to our weakness and failures.

It's a big paradox. Jesus overcame evil through apparent weakness and sacrifice. There was a cosmic battle going on around the cross. Christ was overcoming evil. But it wasn't by lifting up a sword. It was by laying down his life.

> **It was simply an exhortation and a metaphor to get out there—for the Church to rise up and fulfill its destiny.**

Behind the Songs

Shine, Jesus, Shine

Lord, the light of your love is shining,
in the midst of the darkness, shining;
Jesus, Light of the World, shine upon us,
set us free by the truth you now bring us,
shine on me, shine on me.

Shine, Jesus, shine,
fill this land with the Father's glory;
blaze, Spirit, blaze,
set our hearts on fire.
Flow, river, flow,
flood the nations with grace and mercy;
send forth your word, Lord,
and let there be light.

Lord, I come to your awesome presence,
from the shadows into your radiance;
by the blood I may enter your brightness,
search me, try me, consume all my darkness,
shine on me, shine on me.

As we gaze on your kingly brightness,
so our faces display your likeness,
ever changing from glory to glory,
mirrored here may our lives tell your story,
shine on me, shine on me.

Graham Kendrick
Copyright © 1987 Make Way Music

Even the Pope has swung his cane in time to the music!

It was sung at the Dunblane memorial service. It's been used at Billy Graham crusades. It became one of the "folk songs" of Spring Harvest lore. It has remained at the top end of the Church Copyright Licence charts for a decade, and become a standard in schools across the land. Even the Pope has swung his cane in time to the music! "Shine, Jesus, Shine" is one of those songs that just seemed to catch a moment when people were beginning to believe once again that a spiritual impact could be made on an entire nation.

At the time of writing it, Ichthus Christian Fellowship was focusing on the theme of the presence and holiness of God—the God who dwells in unapproachable light. I remember writing the three verses without the chorus and road-testing them. For some reason they weren't quite happening, so the song went back in the file for several months. Later, I came back to a phase of songwriting and I pulled it out again. I quickly concluded that actually this was not a complete song. All it had was three verses—and it needed a chorus.

The phrase "shine, Jesus, shine" came to mind. I think it was one of the quickest things I've ever written! Within 20 minutes or half an hour I'd written the chorus and the whole thing just needed a little bit of editing and tidying up here and there. The chorus fell into place surprisingly naturally. But even then it took a while to mature. I'd written the verses at a different pace. So the tempo of verse and chorus seemed to pull against one another. It was only through use that it actually began to settle down. As I worked on it with my band, an arrangement and a way of doing it took shape. Then it started to feel like a complete song.

It was used at Spring Harvest when it was still very new. And I still had no idea at all of its potential success. I'd written a whole batch of material during that time, and there were other songs that I preferred at the time that are now long forgotten.

I can remember singing it at Spring Harvest, where it became clear that much of the song's dynamics were in the content of that chorus. It's a prayer for the nation. Obviously I'd thought about it—I had the UK in my mind while I was singing it. But because it says "fill this land," it's generic.

So then I started meeting people from other nations who were saying, "This is like our national anthem." Whenever they sang it, they sang it for their own country. I was so glad that I hadn't referred to Britain or England specifically.

It was one of those cases where people were beginning to catch a vision for God doing something on a national level. For my generation, such a widespread spiritual impact had almost seemed too big to contemplate. Decades of decline in the Church had produced a siege mentality, and it had become quite hard to imagine the nation being touched by the gospel. But faith was rising toward that, and the song was carried on a wave of prayer.

"Shine, Jesus, Shine" was new and it caught the spirit of the moment. It was very Jesus-focused. Sometimes when I'm writing songs I ask the question of God, "Can you endorse this song? Is there any reason why you can't put your stamp on it? Is there something about it that fails to expound the truth, exalt Jesus, or offer an emphasis on something important?"

I am always painfully conscious of any compositional or lyrical shortcomings in a song— especially if I see them only when it's too late for changes.

I am always painfully conscious of compositional or lyrical shortcomings in a song—especially if I see them only when it's too late for changes. But I am also aware of how gracious God is to take hold of these faulty vessels and use them, and it's often the case that in the singing of a song, the Spirit of God turns up in a special way. Someone told me about a church in Australia that had become very dry. Very little was happening. But they picked up on "Shine, Jesus, Shine" in its early days. The more they sang it, the more the Spirit of God started to move. I'm sure there were other factors involved, but the story goes that the song brought something new to them. At the very least it seemed that God turned up just when they were singing it!

I find that fascinating. It's something you always want to happen but it's something you can't possibly manufacture. It's something God decides to do. I often wish that I had the knowledge to look into how music presses certain buttons in the heart and mind. But because I've only ever been a play-it-by-ear musician, I've always worked intuitively.

Obviously there is some experience and wisdom that I've picked up along the way in terms of what makes a song work. But at its heart, I guess it's just me trying to do the best that I can and trusting that God is helping me and following it through until I have a complete song.

A key part of my road testing is to submit songs to friends at Ichthus. Faith Forster has been a particularly helpful editor of songs. She and others often point out things that could be a bit clearer, or they help me when I'm stuck and don't know where to take it conceptually. All these things contribute to the songwriting process.

Had I been trying to operate as an isolated individual, a great deal of this just wouldn't have happened. So I've been in a good place. That's not unusual.

Many worship writers are based in a movement or church that has a very definite direction, and all the checks and balances are in place to protect, preserve, and provoke them. All those elements are vital.

Ichthus was pioneering the praise marches before I ever came on board. When I started working with them, I was just giving expression to something they'd already put into place. I was offering my gifts to serve them in that context, to use music to give it more form and structure. Almost inadvertently I created a kind of liturgy for the streets. Suddenly other churches thought, "Oh well, we know how to do it now—here's the simple key, we'll just use that." It worked and they did it. The local church context has been of absolute importance.

Behind the Songs

It must be every songwriter's dream to see their material enjoy a broad connection with huge crowds of people. But there are other dynamics at work when a congregation embraces a particular song: the vocabulary has to sit well in people's mouths; if they feel uncomfortable singing it, it won't work; it can't be so personal to the writer that people can't sing it honestly and identify with it; the melody has to be accessible.

Strange as it may seem, it has probably helped that I don't have an amazingly versatile voice. It tends to take me to solid melodies within a fairly limited range. The chances are that if I'm comfortable singing it, then most people will be comfortable singing it, too.

I've always had a natural attraction to anthems. That might be my background in the hymns. It's been there for as long as I can remember, and that's obviously a great help.

I don't have any formal musical training and often envy people who do. I've learned mainly by trial and error. I take the "hit and miss, try it this way, try it that way, hope for happy accidents" approach. It's probably not the most efficient way of writing songs! But now and again it works. The bottom line is if the song brings a release in my own spirit, perhaps it will produce that in other people, too.

I've had to learn to trust my instincts—and God's prompting. I have to trust that in the process God is helping me to write what will enable other people to worship. I'm not one to claim that a song was given to me straight from heaven. I actually think it's a wonder that God works with us rather than using us as a kind of dictation machine—that he inspires us, helps us, and develops our ability to give.

> **Strange as it may seem, it has probably helped that I don't have an amazingly versatile voice.**

Behind the Songs

What Grace
Worship for a New Millennium

Behind the Songs

No Need to Fear

No need to fear
    when times of trouble come,
        oppression's storm beats at your door,
      no need to fear.

        No need to fear
          though evil seems so strong,
            their pride and power is not for long.

        Be still my soul and trust in God,
      and place your life into his hands,
    for he will never fail you,
  and in the morning you'll see his face,
no need to fear—don't fear.

    No need to fear
      the envy and the scorn
        of those who boast in what they own,
          no need to fear.

          For what remains when life's brief day is done,
        their glories are a setting sun.
      But as for me, of this I'm sure,
    God will redeem my soul from death,
  and he will never fail me,
and in the morning I'll see his face.

What Grace

And he will never fail you,
no one can tear you from his love
and he will never forsake you,
and in the morning you'll see his face,
no need to fear,
don't fear.

Graham Kendrick
Copyright © 1999 Ascent Music

Behind the Songs

As time has gone by, I have appreciated much more than ever Gillian's role in those formative years. She had always been kind and dependable— a godly woman who just got on with quietly serving those around her.

My elder sister Gillian certainly had a part to play in the foundation of all that I do. When you're focused on the creative side of things, you don't want to be bothered with things like answering letters. So Gillian took care of that. If it hadn't been for her, we would never have played anywhere. We just wouldn't have turned up at the right place at the right time!

It was Gillian who used to deal with all the administration for our band in the early days—as well as play keyboards and sing. And as a typical third child, I learned to float along without the sense of responsibility that an eldest child has.

There was a guy called Mick and his wife Mo—known as Mick "n" Mo— who'd taken an interest in the band, and who had a Cortina estate car. We used to pack into this vehicle with all our gear—such as it was—and Mick used to preach as well. Then we recruited a drummer named Martin. He had a job and decided to buy a minibus instead of a car. I think it was the kind of vehicle that used to run around airports or something like that, as it had a revolving orange light on the roof. Being dark blue as well, it would occasionally be mistaken for a police vehicle! The main feature about it was that it would pour out smoke, and used almost as much oil as it did gas. I'm sure it was illegal, but we couldn't afford to get it fixed. So we used to go off on these gigs, leaving a cloud of pollution behind us.

I'd often jump in the minibus on the way to a gig and not have the faintest idea where we were going or what we were doing. Much of the organizing was down to Gillian holding it all together, taking the phone calls, getting the maps, and finding out when we were supposed to arrive there and so on. We couldn't have done it without her.

Sadly, she died in 1988 from cancer. Gillian struggled with the disease for about eight years. It was treated, but then it reappeared. She left a husband and two sons. As time has gone by, I have appreciated much more than ever her role in those formative years. She had always been kind and dependable—a godly woman who just got on with quietly serving those around her.

It's not easy to deal with life-and-death issues in a song. Yet where there is faith in a God who can give eternal life, there is wonderful hope even in the dark times. More recently, while writing songs for *Millennium Chorus*, my attention was drawn to Psalm 49. Out of that flowed the song "No Need to Fear," which was to be sung on the album by Wintley Phipps. He's one of those people whose deep but gentle voice resonates throughout a whole room—just when he's speaking. So Wintley delivers the song powerfully and poignantly, especially the line: "But as for me, of this I'm sure, God will redeem my soul from death."

Just after the recording had been released, a woman took a copy to a friend who was seriously ill in the hospital. She played "No Need to Fear" again and again. This lady had a nominal Christian faith, and she knew she was going to die, but had no assurance of her salvation. Through listening to the song continuously, she came to a place of faith and confidence that she was going to be with the Lord. Wintley Phipps himself heard about this woman's situation, and decided to go and visit her. So Wintley suddenly turned up in her hospital room.

He spent some time with her. And before he left, he decided to sing the song to her, unaccompanied in the hospital room. During the singing of it, she passed away. It was like her final serenade, straight into the arms of Jesus.

What Grace

Behind the Songs

Beauty for Brokenness

Beauty for brokenness,
hope for despair,
Lord, in the suffering,
this is our prayer.
Bread for the children,
justice, joy, peace,
sunrise to sunset
your kingdom increase.

Shelter for fragile lives,
cures for their ills,
work for the craftsmen,
trade for their skills.
Land for the dispossessed,
rights for the weak,
voices to plead the cause
of those who can't speak.

God of the poor, friend of the weak,
give us compassion, we pray,
melt our cold hearts,
let tears fall like rain.
Come, change our love
from a spark to a flame.

What Grace

Refuge from cruel wars,
havens from fear,
cities for sanctuary,
freedoms to share.
Peace to the killing fields,
scorched earth to green,
Christ for the bitterness,
his cross for the pain.

Rest for the ravaged earth,
oceans and streams,
plundered and poisoned,
our future, our dreams.
Lord, end our madness,
carelessness, greed;
make us content with
the things that we need.

Lighten our darkness,
breathe on this flame,
until your justice burns
brightly again;
until the nations
learn of your ways,
seek your salvation
and bring you their praise.

Graham Kendrick
Copyright © 1993 Make Way Music

Behind the Songs

Driving through Bombay in the midnight hour I saw an incredible sight: thousands and thousands of people sleeping out on the streets. Until you see it, you don't really believe it. I even saw laborers unloading a truck, and casually stepping over the top of these street-sleepers. Yet this is how they live. The pavement is their home. Even in the busy traffic the sight of a white face would bring beggars to the open taxi. There were lepers carrying babies, reaching out for rupees with fingerless hands.

You give the rupees, but in the knowledge that the beggars themselves are controlled by Mafia-style setups who take most of the money and keep them at poverty level. They are reputed to deliberately disable people to make them more pitiful, and therefore more effective as beggars. The scale of the poverty and the exploitation felt overwhelming.

From those streets, I returned to England the day before Christmas Eve. Driven by the need to buy presents for friends and family, I found myself in a gift shop in Surrey. Surrounded by trinkets that people don't really need, I found it very hard to cope with the contrast—and was baffled to know how to respond to it all. I don't think I've ever resolved the difference between those two extremes. In the end you have to decide to do what you can do—otherwise you fall into the trap of doing nothing, because it can all seem so futile when the problems are so vast.

Try to deal with that theme in a worship song! Yet that was the challenge facing me when Christian relief agency Tearfund asked if I would write them a song in the run-up to their twenty-fifth anniversary year. After a number of discussions and a fair bit of research, "Beauty for Brokenness" is what came out of it. I went through a lot of Tearfund material and jotted down ideas. I was keen to describe in clear visual imagery the kind of things that their work involved.

I was impressed by the wisdom that Tearfund exercises in the way that they do their work; investing in the long term and attempting to empower people to look after themselves rather than just meet the immediate need, to give people the skills to support themselves and their families. They work through the churches, on the spot where the need

> **I found myself in a gift shop in Surrey. Surrounded by trinkets that people don't really need, I found it very hard to cope with the contrast— and was baffled to know how to respond to it all.**

is, by empowering local Christians to serve their communities. That honors the people. Rather than condescendingly helping out, it empowers them, helps them to develop as a community, and gives them dignity.

In the face of the enormity of the problems, we need vision and faith for change. There are Christians all over the world who've done just that. A British doctor who works in Uganda told our church the story of how several years ago he stood on a field that was empty except for elephant grass. A Christian leader with a vision for meeting the desperate needs of the local people prayed and prophesied over the place. Now on that very field stands a substantial hospital showing God's love through medical care. Vision, faith, prayer, giving, and sheer hard work brought something out of nothing—and hope for thousands.

Hebrews 13:15 talks about the fruit of our lips as a sacrifice of praise to God, using the language and imagery of temple worship. But then it goes on to say, do not neglect to do good and

> **In the face of the enormity of the problems, we need vision and faith for change.**

share what you have because with such sacrifices God is pleased. The latter is received with pleasure by God just as the former is. Both are worship.

Still, it wasn't easy to write a song on this subject, in the context of the praise and worship genre. Living in the affluent West, we have a fair degree of guilt about the fact that other parts of the world are not so well off. But a song that only succeeded in drawing people into a guilt trip would be counter-productive and risk immobilizing them.

So I made the composition focus on God who is the God of the poor and friend of the weak, asking him to give us compassion because we know we don't have very much. Because he is the source of compassion, we can call on him to help us to be like him, and as the song says, to melt our cold hearts and change our love from a spark to a flame. It is saying we have got some concern but, boy, we need a whole lot more. So I was trying to be real and honest and meet us where many of us are. It's a prayer.

Behind the Songs

For This I Have Jesus

For the joys and for the sorrows,
the best and worst of times,
    for this moment, for tomorrow,
    for all that lies behind;
        fears that crowd around me,
        for the failure of my plans,
            for the dreams of all I hope to be,
            the truth of what I am:

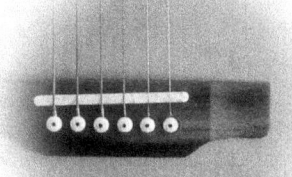

                for this I have Jesus,
                    for this I have Jesus,
                    for this I have Jesus,
            I have Jesus.

        For the tears that flow in secret,
            in the broken times,
      for the moments of elation,
        or the troubled mind;
    for all the disappointments,
      or the sting of old regrets,
all my prayers and longings,
that seem unanswered yet:

What Grace

For the weakness of my body,
the burdens of each day,
      for the nights of doubt and worry
      when sleep has fled away;
           needing reassurance
           and the will to start again,
                a steely-eyed endurance,
                    the strength to fight and win.

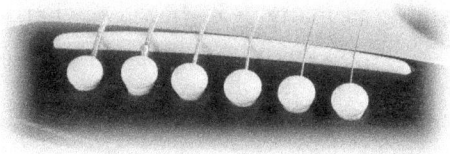

Graham Kendrick

Copyright © 1994 Make Way Music

Behind the Songs

This song was triggered by a line from a sermon. Bible teacher Charles Price was preaching at Spring Harvest in 1994, and illustrated some of the points in his talk by referring to an elderly Christian he knew. For many years his friend had this simple but profound saying that he would apply to whatever came his way, whether challenge or tragedy: "For this I have Jesus."

I was sitting on the platform, because I was leading worship in that meeting. As I listened, I began to see not only the point, but also the potential for a song. So I scribbled down a few thoughts and experimented with a melody in my head. When I had a bit of time back in my room, I started to sketch out the song.

I thought, "Let's make everything build up to this line, 'for this I have Jesus.'" So the song is very much a list of things for which "I have Jesus," that I can identify with, that others can identify with. It's turned out to be one of those songs that encourages people who are going through difficulties, a formula to help them bring their problems to Christ instead of resorting to worrying, fear, and anxiety and blaming other people—which is always what we tend to do when things go wrong.

What Grace

Roy Castle was a popular, successful and very well-respected entertainer. When he died after a long battle with lung cancer, the whole nation was saddened by the news. His wife Fiona seemed to draw from a deep well of strength through that time. She said that "For This I Have Jesus" had "a huge impact" on her when she first heard the song at Spring Harvest 1995, shortly after Roy had died. "It expresses in a beautiful way the value of the relationship we can have with Jesus," she said. "He is with us to help us in every circumstance of our lives."

We all lean on something, particularly when the hard times come. The question is the quality of what we are leaning on. Is it a substitute, a counterfeit, or is it the real thing? The Christian teaching is that we were never made to be simply independent of God, we were made for God, and to find fulfillment in a relationship with him. So without that we are incomplete and we haven't fulfilled the purpose of our existence.

A Belfast woman explained how this composition had been a real encouragement to her after she discovered she had breast cancer—for the second time. "I received a card from a lady at church," she wrote, "and inside she had enclosed the words of the song. I hadn't seen or heard the song before, and I was so thrilled by how they applied to my situation.

"Later that day I received a tape with the song on it. I was so blessed by the way the Lord used this in my situation. I claimed the words as I faced surgery. The words "for the weakness of my body" were very relevant."

But we don't need Jesus just for the bad times. We need him in the good times, too—as the song points out. We need him to cope with success. Success can tempt us to become presumptuous or imagine that somehow we've done something great all by ourselves—as opposed to it really coming from the grace of God. For those times we have Jesus, too, the Jesus who came into his world not to be served, but to serve, and whose greatest success appeared at the time to be a gigantic failure—the cross.

What Grace

Behind the Songs

God Is Great

God is great—amazing!
Come let his praises ring.
God is great—astounding!
The whole creation sings

His clothing is splendor and majesty bright,
for he wraps himself in a garment of light.
He spreads out the heavens, his palace of stars,
and rides on the wings of the wind.

What marvelous wisdom the Maker displays,
the sea vast and spacious, the dolphins and whales.
The earth full of creatures, the great and the small,
he watches and cares for them all.

The rain forest canopies darken the skies,
cathedrals of mist that resound with the choirs
of creatures discordant, outrageous, ablaze
in colorful pageants of praise.

Above his creation the Father presides,
the pulse of the planets, the rhythm of tides,
the moon marks the seasons, the day follows night,
yet he knows every beat of my heart.

Let cannons of thunder salute their acclaim,
the sunsets fly glorious banners of flame,
　　　the angels shout "holy" again and again
　　　as they soar in the arch of the heavens.

Graham Kendrick/Steve Thompson
Copyright © 1993 Make Way Music

**If simple love songs to Jesus, though genuine,
replace the great epic themes and doctrinal statements,
and we neglect to worship God for his creation,
we're missing something that's quite vital, really.**

The theme of creation is a fundamental one—particularly when you want to communicate the gospel to those outside the Church. In many cases it's the starting point. It encapsulates the basic question: where does this all come from? There seems to be marvelous design in nature—is it all just some incredible coincidence, accident, or chance? Or is there an intelligent, personal being behind it all? Of course in his letters, Paul tends to make creation a starting point, that there is a God who made the world.

So it's a foundational theme. Yet it doesn't feature in a great deal of worship material. I regret not having written more, and get regularly nagged by a friend of mine who has spent all his long life working outdoors and delighting with childlike wonder at every aspect of natural creation he encounters. It's something we are tending to neglect in our liturgy—whether that liturgy is written or unwritten—perhaps as a result of urbanization. We've never quite replaced that classic school assembly anthem, "All Things Bright and Beautiful."

Yet the early Christians in Britain and Ireland celebrated and venerated creation. They built their prayer huts and monasteries amid some of the most fantastic scenery on these islands. So they worshipped God using the best visual aid of all—creation itself. In modern times, worship became very personalized. If simple love songs to Jesus, though genuine, replace the great epic themes and doctrinal statements, and we neglect to worship God for his creation, we're missing something that's quite vital, really.

I've never been one of those people who sits in a beautiful place and writes a song about it. For some reason, it doesn't work that way for me. Maybe I'm a "townie" at heart. But I travel a lot. So I see a lot of places—beautiful places. I remember in my younger days visiting North Wales quite a bit. That left a very big impression on me because in my teens I lived in London and I remember getting invited to help out with the music on a school trip, up in North Wales. I developed a great affection for that part of the world—with the remoteness and beauty of it, and the way it changes under the different weather conditions. I'm sure that had something to do with the song "Love Is in the Things You Make," which appeared on the *Paid on the Nail* album back in the mid '70s.

Sometimes, scenes of natural beauty are so strong they leave an indelible impression. I was in California in 1987 for a combined ministry and family

...we have pillaged creation very much because we haven't regarded ourselves as accountable to God for the way we treat his world.

trip. I went for an early morning walk, which is something I've often been in the habit of doing. So off I went down to the beach. Underneath the pastel colors of the morning sky, three dolphins suddenly appeared, swimming in the surf, darting in and out of the waves as they crashed onto the shore. They weren't far from where I was standing. It was a very special moment. I returned to the States three years later for a sabbatical, when I was introduced to the art of snorkelling. It's a whole different world down there, underneath the waves. Trouble is, I don't get much chance to enjoy that kind of experience at home in Croydon!

Many years later, I was inspired to write "God Is Great" after reading Psalm 104, which contains a lot of references to worshipping the Creator by celebrating the kind of things that he's done in nature. The rain forest reference in "God Is Great" was very deliberate. There is so much emphasis on ecology in the wider world these days—which is desperately needed—but what's missing is the whole dynamic of being stewards of creation, answerable to God, who put it into our hands to look after it. There's a big difference between putting man at the center and God at the center. I think our greed has been unrestrained; we have pillaged creation very much because we haven't regarded ourselves as accountable to God for the way we treat his world.

What Grace

Behind the Songs

I Kneel Down

On the bloodstained ground,
where the shadow falls
of a cross and a crown of thorns,
I kneel down, I kneel down.
I lift my eyes to a tear-stained face;
who is this dying in my place?
I kneel down, I kneel down.

    I come just as I am, this is my only plea.
One hope in which I trust, this blood was shed for me.

As you wash the stains of my guilty heart
'til I'm clean in every part,
I kneel down, I kneel down.
Wash away my shame, my pain, my pride,
every sin that I once denied,
I kneel down, I kneel down.

    This is where I'll always come,
        this is where I'll always run, to worship you.
        This is where I'll always come,
            this is where I'll always run,
                to worship you, Jesus.

Graham Kendrick
Copyright © 1998 Ascent Music

When I wrote the first line, "On the Bloodstained Ground," it was more in terms of vividly describing the scene of Christ's death. But after singing it one day, shortly after I had written it, a woman in the crowd told me how the song related to a situation in a way I had never imagined. There had been a murder in her immediate family. One family member had killed another member. One was dead, one had become a murderer. There had been bloodshed and now terrible guilt. The song helped her to go to the cross as the place where God had provided the answer to the horror of bloodshed—through the blood of Christ.

The shadow of the cross falls upon our own bloodstained ground, bringing redemption, healing, and forgiveness to what is otherwise an utterly hopeless situation. Sometimes a few words of description can trigger much more than the writer intended or expected. Such is the power of truth and the poetry of truth, which I search for when I am writing.

I received a letter from a woman in Kent who was carrying the pain of having a "prodigal daughter." The song helped her, too: "As we sang "I Kneel Down," tears began to stream silently down my face. I was overwhelmed by the conviction that it should have been me on that cross, not Jesus." She remarked on 'the feeling of safety and of "coming home."'

The chorus echoes the great hymn "Just as I Am," which traditionally has been sung at evangelistic crusades. I was very conscious of that at the time of writing it, and wondered whether I should change it. But it kind of flowed out that way and though I drafted several alternative lines, I stepped back and thought, "Well, should it go this

Sometimes a few words of description can trigger much more than the writer intended or expected. Such is the power of truth...

way?" And then I thought, "Yes, I think it should." That's the sort of inner debate that goes on in the songwriter's head! For those who know that old song "Just as I Am," there is a very positive resonance with it.

In one sense the language—"this is my only plea"—can seem a little archaic. That is, until you sing it in a prison, which I often do. And there, language like "my only plea" is extremely relevant. And since I wrote this song, I've always included it in my repertoire there. Of course, the words aren't just for those who've committed crimes against society. They have relevance to us all, especially for the day we stand in God's judgment hall and have to give account for all we have said and done.

The song was first recorded on the *Millennium Chorus* project. Graham Ferguson Lacey, a Christian businessman, commissioned me to compose the songs for a musical and visual journey to herald the year 2000. I had already written the song and did not set out to use it there, but there came a point where I looked at it and thought, "Wow—this really fits." So it was brought into the recording.

Billed as "the greatest story ever sung," *Millennium Chorus* was inspired by Jesus' life and message. It consisted of 12 songs performed by such award-winning artists as *Phantom of the Opera* star Michael Crawford and Clannad's lead singer Maire Brennan—together with a host of other class performers. I was well known for taking praise to the streets and now this project was conceived to take worship to the airwaves—through CD, tape, video, DVD, and television broadcasts across the globe.

For people who know me, and what I'm known for, this was different again. It wasn't a praise and worship album, though there was a great spirit of worship to it. It was a song cycle, rather than a musical. We designed it for TV in such a way that you could break it up into individual songs. It was in the style of music videos, but with the emphasis on content rather than just light entertainment.

Because of its intensely confessional nature, "I Kneel Down" really personalized *Millennium Chorus*. The track was placed toward the end of the program, creating a strong focus on the cross as the pivotal moment in not only the world's history but also in the history of our individual lives. I set out tocreate a master plan for the project, but during the period of writing, *Millennium Chorus* really evolved as it went along. That isn't unusual in these kinds of things!

At the time of writing the songs, I didn't know who would be singing them. It was quite a complex process of finding artists who weren't only suitable but also willing, available, and free on the dates to do the recording. There were so many different permutations that I just had to write the songs that I felt inspired to write, and then exercise faith that we'd match songs with singers.

So the whole thing just grew. Then came a point where we laid out all the songs and decided which order they'd go in, with all the usual criteria of style of contrast and flow of ideas and it seemed to fit very well. The fact that "I Kneel Down" is a basically simple, personal worship song that can be sung with an acoustic guitar meant that it suited me. Although originally there was never any intention for me to be an "artist" and sing any of the songs from the album, Graham Lacey felt strongly that I should perform it, and as this piece seemed to fit me so well, that's what we did.

The song reflects the heart of the Gospel. At the cross, we know we are sinners and that our only hope of forgiveness and eternal life is what happened there. Over the years I've heard many of the big, dramatic Christian testimonies that have been published in book form and then retold "live" by the authors themselves at various events and conferences.

Such conversion stories are indeed impressive. But I delight just as much in hearing how very ordinary people meet God for the first time. They're usually the kind of folks that the world would totally ignore and don't even have the distinction of being terrible criminals! But they discover forgiveness and start a personal relationship with God, through Christ, and their lives are transformed. That's where most people are at.

Behind the Songs

I'm Special

I'm special because God has loved me,
for he gave the best thing that he had to save me;
his own Son, Jesus, crucified to take the blame,
for all the bad things I have done.

Thank you, Jesus, thank you, Lord,
for loving me so much.
I know I don't deserve anything,
help me feel your love right now,
to know deep in my heart that I'm your special friend.

Graham Kendrick
Copyright © 1986 Kingsway's Thankyou Music

Elvis Presley and James Dean were busy making their marks on the world. God was just about to make his mark on mine. I must have been about six. My mother was reading a bedtime storybook that quite simply explained forgiveness of sins and giving your life to God and so on. I can remember praying a prayer to that effect once she'd finished the book.

I was conscious that something had happened. I can remember to this day a rush of excitement somewhere inside my chest—which I did not expect. I didn't say anything about it because I didn't have the words to at that sort of age. But I knew my prayer had been answered, that something really significant had happened, and that I had made an important decision. It was a very calm, domestic scene, very matter-of-fact, and the atmosphere was not at all charged.

Then it became a matter of facing the issues as I grew older—even simple moral choices of "do I tell a lie or do I tell the truth?" and "do I admit to my school friends that I am a Christian and risk their ridicule?" and so on. I was able to go to lots of meetings and heard some preachers, and there was always a chance to reaffirm that decision—which I'm sure I did many, many times.

Many years later, I wrote "I'm Special" for a children's event that we had at our church. Every child needs affirmation. But the key thing is, what is the basis of that affirmation? There's an intrinsic value in just being made in the image of God. But the value God puts on us is most dramatically portrayed through the incarnation and through the cross—and God giving the best that he had. So it was just an attempt to encapsulate the Gospel in quite simple childlike language.

One unusual thing about this song is that it's become quite popular, without ever having been recorded on an album, so far as I know. It's been put in songbooks and has found its way around by other means. It's encouraging to know that the "grapevine" is still operational! After all, that is largely how my first worship songs became well known.

I've written very few songs specifically for children, though a lot of songs that weren't written with children in mind became their firm favorites. I know that from my own experience with "Shine, Jesus, Shine." When that song had just emerged, I'd regularly get kids coming up to me with their parents to say that it was their favorite song. Now sometimes I get the same message from those children's children! That always surprised me because "Shine, Jesus, Shine" has three verses as well as a chorus, and is quite wordy. Yet somehow it impacts on children. I've never quite analyzed why.

Undoubtedly there's a special gift to writing children's songs. People like Ishmael are outstanding at this craft.

He makes it a great mixture of fun and teaching and worship. Mixing those three elements together really works. It was surprising to see Ishmael venture into that area.

I knew him when he was with Andy Piercy as Ishmael and Andy, and various other bands like Ishmael United and Rev Counta and the Speedoze—then all of a sudden it was the Glories! My own children went to those early Glories presentations, which presented the gospel in fun, frantic pop songs. It was groundbreaking stuff. Children can so easily be patronized in the Church, but Ishmael introduced something that had a high regard for children's spirituality. He woke people up to the fact that they can really experience God, be filled with the Holy Spirit, and exercise the gifts of the Spirit. A lot of it was to do with honoring, respecting, and valuing children.

It's possible to underestimate how much children relate to what are supposedly "adult" songs. There is also a danger of talking down to children when writing songs for them. Then there is a cutoff age when kids think, "I'm too old to sing that." It's important not to underestimate what they can take in.

Songs can make a powerful impact on our memories. I can recall lots of choruses from my own Sunday school days. There were a couple of songs, for instance, that we always seemed to sing at our church's baptismal services. It was fascinating as a child to witness this spectacle.

My father was the pastor, and he would wear this waterproof suit over his Sunday best that looked like fisherman's waders! They probably were. The carpets were rolled back from the platform, the lid came up, and suddenly this big bath appeared at the front of the church. Then, in the middle of the service, people dressed in white would go down into this bath, ready to be baptized. Just as each person was immersed in the water, we'd sing choruses like "Follow, follow, I will follow Jesus" and "Be faithful unto death." It marked an awesome moment. I wouldn't say they were my favorite choruses, but the circumstances in which they were sung left some of the strongest associations from childhood.

Behind the Songs

Jesus, Restore to Us Again

Jesus, restore to us again
the Gospel of your holy name,
that comes with pow'r, not words alone,
owned, signed, and sealed from heaven's throne.
Spirit and word in one agreed;
the promise to the power wed.

*The word is near, here in our mouths
and in our hearts, the word of faith;
proclaim it on the Spirit's breath:
Jesus!*

Your word, O Lord, eternal stands,
fixed and unchanging in the heavens.
The Word made flesh to earth came down
to heal our world with nail-pierced hands.
Among us here you lived and breathed,
you are the message we received.

Spirit of truth, lead us, we pray,
into all truth as we obey.
And as God's will we gladly choose,
your ancient power again will prove
Christ's teaching truly comes from God,
he is indeed the living Word.

What Grace

Upon the heights of this our land
with Moses and Elijah stand.
Reveal your glory once again,
show us your face, declare your name.
Prophets and law, in you, complete
where promises and power meet.

Grant us in this decisive hour
to know the Scriptures and the power;
the knowledge in experience prove,
the power that moves and works by love.
May word and works join hands as one,
the word go forth, the Spirit come.

Graham Kendrick
Copyright © 1992 Make Way Music

Behind the Songs

> It's quite a wordy piece. It could be argued that if I'd written a shorter, catchier song around the same theme, it might have been more effective, but I guess I found so many "pearls," I couldn't resist stringing them all together!

A quiet revolution was underway. A number of people had been exploring the whole idea of marrying Word and Spirit, drawing together the great teaching tradition of the evangelical community with the powerful prophetic emphasis of the charismatic movement. That phase of the Church's development was reflected in the most unlikely alliance between R. T. Kendall, pastor of Westminster Chapel, and Paul Cain, one of the so-called "Kansas City prophets."

The story goes that they recognized in each other what was missing in their own lives. According to Pentecostal church leader Colin Dye, R. T. Kendall said to Paul Cain, "I need your power," to which the other responded, "I need your theology." Out of that, a friendship emerged between them, and not a little controversy!

It was R. T. Kendall himself who provided the motivation for my song "Jesus, Restore to Us Again." He'd been very concerned about the relationship between the Spirit and the Word—obviously from his own knowledge and experience of biblical exposition and spiritual renewal. He'd been chatting with Paul Cain, and out of that he came to me and said, "We really need a song that brings together the Spirit and the Word." In my usual way I did a study of scriptures where those two things seemed to come together. After writing the song, I introduced it at the Word and Spirit Conference at London's Wembley Conference Centre in October 1992, where I also led the worship at the evening celebration.

It's quite a wordy piece. It could be argued that if I'd written a shorter, catchier song around the same theme, it might have been more effective, but I guess I found so many "pearls," I couldn't resist stringing them all together! But there you go. When you write a song, you have to go with what comes. I have to admit that one of my faults as a songwriter is trying to fit too much in. But the dilemma is that as you dig into the Word, you find so much to say and you look at it all and you think, "Well, which verse do I throw out, there is so much wonderful truth here?" Still, R. T. was pleased with it, and he reprinted the lyrics in the book he wrote with Paul Cain, simply entitled *The Word and the Spirit* (Struik/Kingsway, 1996).

I used Moses and Elijah as symbolic of Word and Spirit. They were not contemporaries, but in the account of Christ's transfiguration they meet and speak with him. Hence, "Upon the heights of this our land/with Moses and Elijah stand"—so that we see Word and Spirit brought together in Christ and impacting on the nation. For those who might be concerned about comparisons with William Blake's poetry, it's not quite the same as "And did those feet in ancient times"! Call it poetic license!

> "When the Word and the Spirit come together, there will be the biggest movement of the Holy Spirit that the nation, and indeed the world, has ever seen."
>
> SMITH WIGGLESWORTH

I do believe that in recent times those who emphasize the Word of God, and those who emphasize the Spirit of God, have become more open to one another. No one stream, denomination, or church has got it all. But if we can build relationship and respect and learn from one another, then we are much more likely to find balance. The lyrics reflect that challenge quite specifically, so it's not a song you would use in every worship time. But when that theme is on the agenda, it comes into its own.

The "background noise" to all this was the legendary "revival prophecy" about Spirit and Word coming together, traditionally attributed to the famous revivalist Smith Wigglesworth: "When the Word and the Spirit come together, there will be the biggest movement of the Holy Spirit that the nation, and indeed the world, has ever seen. It will mark the beginning of a revival that will eclipse anything that has been witnessed within these shores, even the Wesleyan and the Welsh revivals of former years. The outpouring of God's Spirit will flow over from the UK to the mainland of Europe, and from there will begin a missionary move to the ends of the earth." Whatever one believes about that prophecy, it remains that because the Word and the Spirit are seen together in Christ, and they should be seen together in his Church.

What Grace

Behind the Songs

No Scenes of Stately Majesty

No scenes of stately majesty for the King of kings.
    No nights aglow with candle flame for the King of love.
        No flags of empire hung in shame for Calvary.
            No flowers perfumed the lonely way that led him to
                a borrowed tomb for Easter Day.

No wreaths upon the ground were laid for the King of kings.
    Only a crown of thorns remained where he gave his love.
        A message scrawled in irony—"King of the Jews"—
            lay trampled where they turned away, and no one knew
                that it was the first Easter Day.

Yet nature's finest colors blaze for the King of kings.
    And stars in jeweled clusters say: "Worship heaven's King."
        Two thousand springtimes more have bloomed—
            is that enough?
                Oh, how can I be satisfied until he hears
                    the whole world sing of Easter love?

What Grace

My prayers shall be a fragrance sweet for the King of kings.
    My love the flowers at his feet for the King of love.
        My vigil is to watch and pray until he comes.
            My highest tribute to obey and live to know
                the power of that first Easter Day.

I long for scenes of majesty for the risen King.
    For nights aglow with candle flame for the King of love.
        A nation hushed upon its knees at Calvary,
            where all our sins and griefs were nailed
                and hope was born of everlasting Easter Day.

Graham Kendrick

Copyright © 1997 Ascent Music

London was shrouded in deep sorrow. Flowers covered the pavements. Candlelit vigils were held in the streets. People cried out as the solemn procession went by. They were extraordinary scenes. As I watched the TV coverage of Princess Diana's funeral, I was trying to work out in my mind what was going on. There was something quite religious in it all. But it wasn't God-focused or Christ-centered. What we did see were huge numbers of the population trying to come to terms with their shock and grief at the death of an icon.

It was very strange to hear Elton John sing "Candle in the Wind" in a religious environment. Despite being altered lyrically, the song still carried all those associations with Marilyn Monroe—the tragic heroine, the film star, the sex symbol. Whatever one thinks about Diana, the events around her funeral did illustrate that although there's very little residual understanding of the Christian faith in this nation anymore, there is a tremendous yearning for meaning in the face of death, a latent spiritual hunger that materialism and individualism haven't even remotely satisfied.

I wanted to respond to it in some way as a songwriter. After one or two failed attempts at a composition, what began to strike me was the contrast between this funeral that had become a global telecast via the media, and the funeral—or rather the lack of a funeral—of Jesus the King of kings. So I guess the first line set me off in the direction of that contrast: "No scenes of stately majesty." And then I deliberately began to draw in the imagery of the candles, flags at half-mast, the scent of flowers, wreaths and handwritten messages, and so on—and that became the imagery of the song.

> **There is a tremendous yearning for meaning in the face of death, a latent spiritual hunger that materialism and individualism haven't even remotely satisfied.**

In the third verse I took the perspective out wider to the fact that although his death was ignored by the authorities, nature gives him glory. Christ—through whom the world was made—is given praise and honor by nature's finest colors and stars in jeweled clusters. The reference to "2,000 springtimes" built on that imagery and brought in a millennial theme. So it's a kind of intuitive journey exploring those contrasts.

A fifth verse, not on the recording and in the "optional" category, ends with a yearning to see scenes like that again—but this time for Christ. That's where it all took me. Here was this incredible spiritual hunger that wasn't satisfied. And there was no hope of resurrection, only the futility of a young life cut tragically short. That produced a longing within me to see candlelit vigils of repentance and forgiveness and offerings of worship to Jesus on that kind of scale.

Some may think it unusual for me to write a song like that. I'm known for exploring biblical themes, making sure the content's right and that it displays the right balance. But this time it's a visual journey laden with a lot of imagery. I'm not sure how deliberate I am with that process. The truth is, I tend to be rather disorganized in my songwriting. Having brainstormed lots of ideas, the biggest challenge for me is then to actually put them into some sort of order and create something out of the chaos. It often starts with an intuitive journey but then I have to look for the shape—both from the theological and the musical angle.

For the musical setting, I chose a Celtic style. In fact, that's the direction it took from the first line. I guess like most writers, a lot of ideas come just from experimenting, trying it this way and that way—and then finding something that seems to fit the lyric particularly well. Then you build on that. This song started with the first line, and everything else flowed out of that.

I've long been attracted to the Celtic style of music for worship. There's a melancholy to it, and I have always had a melancholic streak. So that appeals to me. And of course the subject matter is melancholic. Also it's a style that has become very popular and it can carry content.

I often reflect on the fact that the genre of worship choruses is largely derived from a three-and-a-half-minute pop song, which isn't designed to carry great content. It's designed to carry simple emotion. That puts a limit on how much content that style of music can carry.

The Celtic hymn style can carry much more content and as it has gained in popularity, people are more willing to sing something with that kind of melody. That's evident by the fact that a lot of old hymns are being sung again to Celtic-style tunes, such as "I Heard the Voice of Jesus Say" and "Be Thou My Vision." Diana was Princess of Wales—a Celtic nation—so the style fitted in that context, too. The fact that the song was included on the *Millennium Chorus* album was also interesting, because the inspiration came from what will forever be seen as an epic moment in the story of modern Britain.

Maire Brennan, lead singer of Celtic rock band Clannad, was chosen to sing the track. Although I missed out on the actual vocal recording session, I have worked with her since on several occasions and have been impressed not only by her beautiful singing, but also by her genuine Christian faith.

Behind the Songs

This Is the Year

Can you feel what I'm feeling?
        Can you hear what I hear?
There's a new day dawning,
a new sound in the air.
        We've been waiting
   for the healing,
and surely the time is here.

This is the year when hearts go free
        and broken lives are mended,
I hear the sound of Jubilee,
   the song of sorrow ended.
This is the year, this is the year.

There's a cry in the darkness,
        there's a child all alone,
   where is love and mercy?
Why are hearts like stone?
        But there's a hush of sacred things,
   the brush of angel wings,
as heaven comes breaking through.

What Grace

*This is the year of joy for tears
    and beauty out of ashes.
When skies will clear if we will share,
    forgive and learn what love is.
        Let's crown the year with kindness
    and live in peace;
fill all the world with songs
        that never cease.*

*This is the year when hearts go free
    and broken lives are mended.
I hear the sounds of Jubilee,
    the song of sorrow ended.
This is the year, this is the year.*

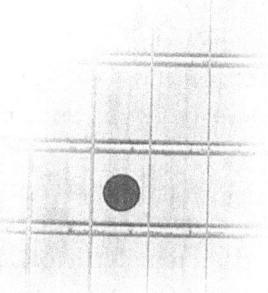

Graham Kendrick
Copyright © 1998 Ascent Music

Jubilee was an epic moment. It was the occasion in Bible times when liberty was proclaimed throughout the land. The word came to prominence recently with the emergence of the Jubilee 2000 campaign—itself inspired by scripture—which called for the rich nations to cancel third world debts and give a new start to the world's poor.

"This Is the Year" set out to capture a sense of joyful anticipation of that strategic time from scripture. I wrote it as part of the commission for the *Millennium Chorus.* On the album it's sung by Jennifer Holiday, who first came to fame on Broadway in the '80s. She has a wonderful ability for putting across a song. When you watch her sing it on the accompanying video, you just can't ignore her delivery. Every word is savored and powerfully communicated.

Inspiration for the words goes back to one of my often-visited scripture passages, which is Isaiah 61. Jesus quoted it and applied it to himself in the synagogue in Nazareth as reported in Luke 4. It describes Jubilee, the season in the ancient Jewish calendar where debts were forgiven, slaves were set free, and people returned to their inheritance. It was a kind of social and economic cycle. It was the fiftieth year and it was there to restore justice and to give people another chance to start again—all those very positive things. Jesus applied that to himself at the beginning of his ministry.

For me, it's one of the Bible's most inspiring visions. It was announced in the Old Testament with the blowing of a trumpet. So there was a wonderful music connection—and it expresses the heart of what the gospel is. I've gone to that scripture several times as a songwriter, but this time, rather than turn it into a praise and worship song, I was looking for a song that would be performed.

It seemed to fit the Millennium year, in the sense of the new dawn and new beginning. It's an announcement, a proclamation of hope—the hope that is fulfilled in Christ. So if you put this side by side with Isaiah 61, you will find the resonances.

Having written the performance version, I then wrote another verse that became part of the finale of the *Millennium Chorus*. Then I saw the possibility of taking three verses and turning it into a congregational hymn. So it actually exists in two versions—the one printed here that is for solo performance and one that can be sung congregationally.

Of course, the phrase "this is the year" is not referring to a calendar year but to an age of the Church. In the Old Testament it was literally a 12-month year or whatever the Jewish calendar was at the time, and then the cycle would go around another 50 years. But when Jesus took it on his lips, it became a whole era that has since continued for 2,000 years. We're still in that era now. We're still in the year of the Lord's favor. God continues to show his favor through Christ, who is the fulfillment of all these things, and sets the prisoners free.

The lovely thing about it is that Jubilee is about the complete transformation of society, a reminder that salvation is holistic and applies to body, mind, and spirit, to politics and economics. Unfortunately, spirituality has been separated off into an abstract dimension. But the true Judeo-Christian slant on it is holistic. That's one of the things I've really appreciated, being a part of Ichthus Christian Fellowship. It is a church committed to preaching a holistic gospel—not just a spiritual one of private beliefs.

Behind the Songs

What Grace

Father, to you with songs of love we come
    into your presence in awe of all you've done,
        brought here with joy before your throne of grace
            and in the Son you love given our place.

What grace to be found in him,
heaven's glorious King.
Father, what grace raising us to life,
choosing us in Christ.
Father, what grace.

Deep is the joy that fills your courts above,
while angels wonder at your redeeming love,
and as you gaze with joy upon your Son,
your eyes are on the ones his love has won.

No higher call than to be heirs with him,
    so let our passion burn for heavenly things.
Seated with Christ for him alone to live,
our hearts forever where our treasure is.

Graham Kendrick
Copyright © 2001 Make Way Music

Behind the Songs

Philip Yancey thought it might end his career in certain circles. But when he wrote *What's So Amazing About Grace?*, it scooped a major award. He'd included extensive references to a leading gay activist, and President Bill Clinton—neither of them heroic figures among Christians in the States. Yet still the book earned him an honor. As Yancey himself said, "It looks like I underestimated the power of grace."

Like many others, I had been reading Yancey's book and found it very helpful. When it came around to compiling the tracks for my most recent album, the theme of God's grace ran through many of the songs. It wasn't so much a theological treatise as a heart response to grace in the whole Gospel—the undeserved favor that God shows us. It seemed to sum up the spirit of the project, so we named it after one of the tracks, "What Grace."

Following the couple of years spent on the *Millennium Chorus*, I was keen to get back to recording an album of praise and worship songs for the Church. I wanted to provide material that was Christ-focused and strongly based on scripture. As I talked to various people in church leadership and many who led worship, I found a hunger for songs that are very much focused on the Lord, his qualities and his attributes. Some felt there were too many songs that are subjective, experiential, and individualistic.

Quite a number of songs on *What Grace* are very clearly based on particular scriptures. I very much believe that a large part of our worship is singing truth. So I bore that in mind more than ever as I wrote that material. That is not to say that experience songs are not important. It's more a matter of balance. We worship in spirit and in truth, and I was sensing a growing hunger for more songs that are truth-packed, and that are concerned with the divine testimony of who God is and what he has revealed to us.

There was a tangible sense of God's grace in the production of the album itself. Behind the scenes, we have been able to draw together different generations of worship leaders, songwriters, and musicians. So the recording has become a tangible expression of the importance of mutual respect and working together. Matt Redman and Martin Smith—two key songwriters from the emerging generation—agreed to sing on one track each. And Andy Piercy, a friend and colleague from the heady days of Christian festivals, has produced the whole album. Andy formerly worked as one half of the zany duo Ishmael and Andy, and then went on to become frontman for the rock band After the Fire, who enjoyed some chart success in the '70s.

Malachi 4:6 says, "And he shall turn the heart of the fathers to the children, and the heart of the children to their fathers." That way, the blessings of one generation can be passed on to the next. It's not a matter of one goes out, one comes in. It's all about walking together and trying to make sure that the next generation doesn't start from ground zero, but can build on the gains of the previous generation. That's just as an important issue in worship as in any other aspect of church life.

> **We worship in spirit and in truth, and I was sensing a growing hunger for more songs that are truth-packed, and that are concerned with the divine testimony of who God is and what he has revealed to us.**

Behind the Songs

Lord, You've Been Good to Me

Lord, you've been good to me,
all my life, all my life.
Your loving kindness never fails.
I will remember all you have done.
bring from my heart
thanksgiving songs.

New every morning is your love
filled with compassion from above.
Grace and forgiveness full and free,
Lord, you've been good to me.

So may each breath I take
be for you, Lord, only you.
Giving you back the life
Love so amazing,
mercy so free,
Lord, you've been good,
so good to me.

Graham Kendrick
Copyright © 2001 Make Way Music

After the frantic schedule that is just about every household's morning routine, there was a welcome stillness in our home. And I was alone in my worship. I was thinking back on God's goodness to me thoughout my life. I began to sing out my thoughts. Although the usual crafting of lyric, melody, and chords followed (in fact, I was still choosing from alternative lines at the microphone in the studio!), the essence of the song "Lord, You've Been Good to Me" was captured in that moment.

It seems a fitting lyric with which to conclude this collection of songs, memories, and reflections. The words look both backward and forward—backward in thanksgiving and forward in anticipation of faithful love that is, as Jeremiah the prophet expressed it, new every morning.

I have called this book *Behind the Songs* and attempted to give the reader a glimpse of the stories and circumstances of their writing. Now and again, however, there comes a reminder of the way that God can take something as simple as words fitted to a melody, crafted in the most mundane of circumstances and in the shadow of the writer's weakness and inadequacy, yet make it live and breathe and become part of some other worshipper's story. Just this morning, as I sat down to write these final paragraphs around the words of this song, a letter was handed to me. The family who sent it have kindly given me their permission to share it with you.

What Grace

Our family are members of a church in Buckinghamshire and a friend gave me your new CD, *What Grace*, about a week ago.

Our son, Joshua, aged 8, very recently died after the sudden onset of a brain tumor, which has been a devastating loss to us, our relatives, our church, and the whole community. Without going into details, there has also been tremendous blessing and God has answered prayer in many remarkable ways. We were allowed to use a large Anglican church in the centre of town for Joshua's Thanksgiving, which was held yesterday and attended by 500-plus adults and children.

Your song "Lord, You've Been Good to Me" started to become our cry last week as we reflected on the goodness of God, and the line about bringing out thanksgiving from our hearts meant a lot. We decided to play it yesterday as our friends arrived for the service and it filled the church with truth and light and the presence of God.

We wanted you to know how much it helped us. Many of our friends commented afterwards about the beautiful music and, of course, countless hearts were moved and there were many tears.

On your video interview you mentioned your hope that the songs would be used, and yesterday we certainly saw the impact on many folk who do not know Jesus. Thank you so much.

It takes me back to one of the first stories of Jesus that impacted on me as a small child. I pictured myself as the lad who brought his packed lunch of bread and fish to Jesus and watched in amazement as he blessed it, broke it, and multiplied it enough to satisfy the hunger of five thousand men and their families, with twelve basketfuls of scraps left over for good measure.

When any of us bring what we have in our hand, though it may seem very little, Jesus accepts it and delights to do miracles with it. It doesn't always result in something that goes public, as songs do by their very nature. But the reward will be the same, if not greater, on the day of reckoning.

If you are among those who sing my songs as you worship God, all I can say is thank you, I feel deeply honored. But the real privilege for us all is to count ourselves as fellow pilgrims on this journey into the heart of worship.

What Grace

Index of Songs

Breaking of the Dawn
Long as I Live   19
How Much Do You Think You Are Worth?   24
Kingdom Come 30
Sweet Fire   36
The Executioner   42
Peter at the Breaking of the Bread   46

God Put a Fighter in Me
Fighter 54
Jesus, Stand Among Us 60
The Blame   68
Anywhere You Walk   74
Bad Company   76
Nicodemus   82
The Servant King   87
There's a Sound on the Wind (Battle song)   91

Carnival of Praise
This Is My Beloved Son 96
The Candle Song   103
Earth Lies Spellbound   109
Let the Flame Burn Brighter (We'll Walk the Land)   115

Index of Songs

We Believe   123
Lord, Have Mercy on Us   129
Meekness and Majesty   134
O Lord, the Clouds Are Gathering   140
Rejoice! Rejoice!   146
Shine, Jesus, Shine   151

What Grace

No Need to Fear   160
Beauty for Brokenness   166
For This I Have Jesus   172
God Is Great   178
I Kneel Down   185
I'm Special   191
Jesus, Restore to Us Again   196
No Scenes of Stately Majesty   202
This Is the Year   208
What Grace   213
Lord, You've Been Good to Me   217

www.ingramcontent.com/pod-product-compliance
Lightning Source LLC
Chambersburg PA
CBHW051351070526
44584CB00025B/3717